Soapmaking

A
Magickal
Guide

By
Alicia Grosso

New Page Books
A division of The Career Press, Inc.
Franklin Lakes, NJ

SOAPMAKING
EDITED BY CLAYTON W. LEADBETTER
TYPESET BY EILEEN DOW MUNSON
Cover design by Lu Rossman/Digi Dog Design
Printed in the U.S.A. by Book-mart Press

To order this title, please call toll-free 1-800-CAREER-1 (NJ and Canada: 201-848-0310) to order using VISA or MasterCard, or for further information on books from Career Press.

The Career Press, Inc., 3 Tice Road, PO Box 687,
Franklin Lakes, NJ 07417
www.careerpress.com
www.newpagebooks.com

Library of Congress Cataloging-in-Publication Data

Grosso, Alicia.
    Soapmaking : a magickal guide / by Alicia Grosso.
        p. cm.
    Includes index.
    ISBN 1-56414-648-0 (pbk.)
    1. Magic. 2. Soap—Miscellanea. I. Title.

BF1623.S55 G76 2003
133.4'4—dc21

2002071915

Dedicated to the readers of this book—
many blessings
as you undertake this
new magickal adventure.

Many thanks to—

The vast, warm, and extremely helpful online community of soapmakers, drawn together around the virtual soap pot.

Fellow soapers Suzanne Buckles, Charlon Bobo, Barbara Hardy, Sue Smith, RuthAnn Wachsmuth, and Misty Simon.

My grandmothers and great-grandmothers who taught me the beauty of handcrafting.

The Sisterhood of Avalon, Students of Ancient Religions, Long Beach Womanspirit.

My great circle of family and friends who have provided encouragement and "human testing."

The people who've contributed to the Collective past, present, and future, including: Jennifer Rivera, Alison Lister, Jennifer Mosier, Marc Studer, Nancy Grant, David Grant, Eleanor Arthur, and Gwendolyn Davis.

Rachel Fain, for boundless love and everything else.

Clayton Leadbetter, who really gets it.

Jacky Sach, for believing in the magick of soap.

Julianna Rees—the real Annabella.

John Rivera, my favorite person.

Disclaimer

The contents of this book are accurate and complete to the best of my knowledge. The information provided should not be taken as medical advice or used as a substitute for medical treatment. All recommendations are made without guarantee on the part of the author or New Page Books. Recipes in the book may not be used for commercial purposes. The author and publisher disclaim any liability in connection with the use of this information.

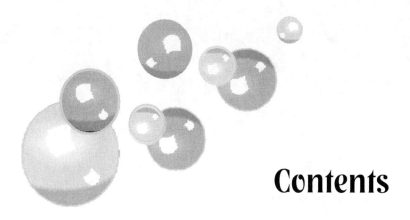

Contents

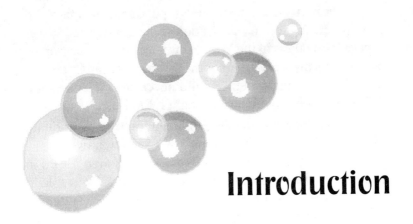

Introduction

This book came about due to an intersection of two major forces in my life. I am a professional soapmaker. I am also a Witch. I find that these two facets of existence continually intertwine and have blended together to create my practice of Magickal Soapmaking.

I began making soap as part of a small craft project to keep myself busy and perhaps earn some extra money during one of the few summers I was neither in school nor teaching summer school. I created a line of products for gardeners based on my longtime interest in herbs. Part of that line is an amazing soap made with herbs and essential oils. I became so entranced with the soapmaking process that I wanted to make more kinds of soap. In fact, I couldn't stop thinking about making soap—I was hooked! As I wanted to keep the group of products for gardeners limited, I expanded and created an ever-changing, ever-growing line of handmade soaps.

Around the same time, I found myself "coming out of the broom closet." Although I'd never made a secret of my spiritual practices, I wasn't completely open about it either. I'd been a practicing solitary since adolescence, and have "Water Witches" and others of the Wise in my ancestry. It is a certainty, however, that my great-grandmothers, who were gardeners and always had a home remedy, would never have tolerated the "W" word. They would have thought it foolish.

I left Washington state for Los Angeles to go to graduate school. Moving to a large urban area, from a relatively rural setting, was a great shock to my system. Although I lived in the suburbs and cities of the Pacific Northwest, I was able to see the Cascade and Olympic mountains and the Puget Sound every day and get to them within minutes. As a little girl, I spent enormous amounts of time in the woods and at the beach, virtually in my own backyard and sometimes in very remote and wild areas. The seasons, the turn of the Great Wheel, are easy to see where I grew up. The Great Mother's ever-shifting raiment is obvious in the cycles of rain, snow, falling leaves, and blue skies.

I suppose you don't really test your commitment to a way of thinking until that way of thinking becomes difficult. I found myself more and more disconnected from Her in the wilds of Los Angeles. I heard myself saying how much I hated the land here, the barrenness, the heat, the lack of obvious seasons, the ugliness of the out-of-control development. Although I lived only miles from Mamma Ocean, I rarely went to see her. Unhappy with my self-induced disconnection from the Mother, I decided to make a change in my attitude by embracing Her here. I "came out" as a Witch, and began to make myself see Her beauty in what I had been experiencing as a hostile environment. There are, of course, seasons here in southern California, however subtle in comparison to more northern climes. Mundane chores like working on composting, and growing herbs, flowers, and food in my urban backyard gave me a direct feel for the turn of the Wheel. Carrying out magickal workings openly in my backyard and in my home helped create the connection.

As I openly and more fully embraced my growing spiritual practices, the despair lessened, and I began to find and embrace the beauty of my new home. I cannot say that even now, after 10 years, I am not lonely for the dark forests and rocky beaches of the Puget Sound. However, I find daily beauty and richness, subtle and obvious evidence of the Great Mother, in this vast southern California desert.

When I started making herbal formulas, I used information from my study of herbs in mundane as well as Craft-related matters. I began to make soaps and other things for myself for purification before ritual. As I became more and more involved with soapmaking, I found making the soap to be a ritual in itself. The discipline of research, preparation, combination, and patience that goes into making soap is very similar to the discipline of ritual and magick. Combining discreet elements to create a new, distinct substance is not alchemy, per se, but there is certainly an alchemical element to it.

Over the years I have put together a number of procedures, recipes, correspondences, and rituals that make up my practice of Magickal Soapmaking, shared here with you. This book is not a complete course in making soap, nor is it a course in magick. It may be a starting place for your further studies into soapmaking, magick, or both.

As you would with any magickal practice new to you, carefully read the information and directions. Have a goal when you begin. Be careful with potentially hazardous lye, and take joy in disciplining yourself to use it with care. Focus on learning the basic procedures, then let your creativity flow and create beautiful, useful soaps for magickal purposes and to add a measure of that magick to your daily life.

Many Blessings,
Alicia

P.S. If you are not a "magickal" person, don't despair at finding this book. There is nothing "bad" here. Modern magick is all about loving Earth and Her plant and animal inhabitants. If you wish to know more about Witchcraft, Earth Religions, and Neo-Paganism, go online, to the bookstore, and to the library. The ever-growing magickal community is rich, beautiful, and vibrant.

PART ONE:

Preparation and Instructions for Making Your Magickal Soap

In Chapter 1, you will find information about keeping a Soap Grimoire and all of the basic equipment and ingredients you need to start making magickal soap. There are charts listing many of the essential oils, herbs, flowers, and other additives you can incorporate into your soaps, as well as their significance to the magickal intent and other properties.

Chapter 2 presents the soapmaking process step by step, providing the basic fundamentals needed to create all of the specialized recipes in Part Two, and others of your own design. You'll learn about the various stages of the soap and how to approach each part of the procedure.

Finally, the ritual elements of soapmaking are explored in Chapter 3, showing you how various steps in the soapmaking process translate into ritual, based on your own tradition and practices.

Chapter 1

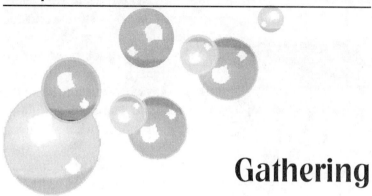

Gathering

Collecting equipment and ingredients is the first step in learning the basics. The recipes in this book are for small batches you can make with tools you probably already have in your kitchen. If your interest expands beyond the scope of this book, there are many fine soapmaking texts listed in Appendix F.

Soap Grimoire

As a magickal person, you may already keep a Book of Shadows. This is where you record all your magickal workings. These books can be simple or elaborate, according to your desire and tradition. There is often another book, especially for herbs, recipes, and potions, called a Grimoire.

I strongly suggest that you keep another book, just for your Magickal Soapmaking. Call this your Soap Grimoire. Record all of your soapmaking activities. One of the most frequent complaints made by soapmakers is that they just can't remember how to make "that wonderful soap" that they created on the spur of the moment. Keep track of your shopping, the good stores, and the helpful woman at the magick shop. Keep track of when you made each batch of soap, and not only what went into it, but the important planetary positions, your mood, and what was going on in the house. Record your intentions, spellwork, poems, songs, etc. that you used while making the soap.

Example of possible Soap Grimoire cover

As you make more and more soap, you'll find you're writing your own soap book. It is a wonderful feeling, to go back over the early batches, see how you learned from your mistakes, and notice how you came up with something wonderfully original. Remember that everything happens for a reason. You may have forgotten an essential oil you'd planned on adding and found that the soap is better, new, or unique without it.

In Appendix I, you'll find a chart to follow when making your Soap Grimoire entries. Use the format I've given you, then, if you like, change it to fit your growing experience. No matter how you wind up keeping your records, just be sure to do it!

Infusions

So many wonderful things humans have created have come spontaneously into being. Soap itself may have been discovered "by accident."

One of the many stories about the origins of soapmaking takes place on the river below Mount Sappo. Burnt offerings of animals were made to the Gods on the mountain. Women cleaning clothes downstream found that there was a special quality to the water there that made their cleaning chores easier. The fats from the animals were washed through the ashes of the fires, making a crude soap.

Equipment

These are the basic items you will need for small-batch soapmaking. Use these items, along with the instructions in Chapter 2, a number of times, until you get a feel for other things you might like to use. If you decide to do a great deal of soapmaking, you can go to thrift stores to obtain low-cost equipment you can dedicate just to soapmaking.

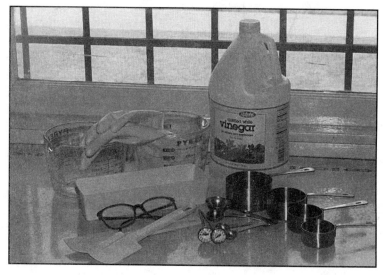

Equipment

- Scale that weighs in .25-ounce increments, has a "tare" or set-to-zero setting, and can weigh up to 10 pounds.

- Two 4-cup, heat-proof, glass measuring cups.

- Two "easy-read" thermometers.

- Two 1-piece, silicone spatulas or wooden spoons. I love the look and feel of wooden spoons, but they get "eaten" by the lye after awhile. One-piece silicone spatulas are best if you want something durable.

- Measuring cups and spoons. Use stainless steel as it won't react with the ingredients.

- Disposable plastic cup.

- Rubber gloves. *Always* wear gloves when handling lye and uncured soap. If you have a question as to whether or not the soap is still caustic, err on the side of caution.

- Eye protection. Your own glasses will work if they have big lenses, but your safest bet is plastic goggles. You can buy them at hardware stores.

- White vinegar. It will help neutralize any lye or raw soap splashed on skin. Keep it close at hand. You may put some in a labeled spray bottle. Use it also as a cleanup aid.

- Heat-proof, flexible plastic containers to use for soap molds. Rubbermaid makes drawer organizers that are perfect for the recipes in this book. They are usually white or cream colored and come in a range of sizes. Larger baby-wipe containers are perfect, as are the containers from some facial or personal cleansing cloths. Make sure your mold can hold 24 fluid ounces. Also, be certain that the containers you choose are dishwasher safe and flexible. If you can run your prospective mold through the dishwasher, it will withstand the heat generated by curing soap. The mold must be flexible so you can push the soap out with ease.

- Old towel to insulate the soap in the mold during the 48-hour insulation period.

- Other items include: glass bowls of varying sizes, mortar and pestle for crushing seeds and herbs, small spatulas, bamboo skewers, chop sticks.

For a quick-reference checklist of the equipment listed here, consult Appendix A.

———————

"Can I make soap without lye?"

In short, no. All soap comes from a chemical reaction between fatty acids—oils—and a strong alkali or base—sodium hydroxide or lye. Cold process soapmaking, which is the technique used in this book, is just one way of making soap.

When the chemical reaction is complete, there is no lye left in the soap. The base and the fatty acids combine to make glycerin and soap molecules. The soap will become less and less alkaline as it ages.

———————

If you want to create soap, but don't want to handle the lye, you can work with a technique called soap casting. This process involves the use of meltable "glycerine" soaps. There are many kinds available, from nearly transparent to opaque, and soaps enriched with substances such as olive oil and goats milk. You simply melt the blocks of soap, add color, scent, and other materials, and then pour it into molds. To give this wonderful craft a try, go to your craft store where you will find a widening array of melt-and-pour soapmaking supplies. To learn more, you can also check out *Soothing Soaps: for Healthy Skin* (Interweave Press, 1997), by Sandy Maine.

Ingredients

The following ingredients make the Basic Recipe for this book. The oils are easily obtained and make very nice soap with rich, creamy foam.

Oils and lye

- **Olive Oil**—Use the less expensive kind (it doesn't have to be labeled "virgin"). Read the label and make sure it's 100% olive oil and not a blend. This oil contributes cleansing and foaming properties. It will range in color from light yellow to medium green.

- **Coconut Oil**—available in 12-ounce jars at natural food stores in the cosmetic department. Coconut oil is white and solid at room temperature.

- **Castor Oil**—Find it in the laxative section in the drug store and in the cosmetics section of the natural food store.

- **Filtered or Distilled Water**—If there are minerals and excessive chlorine in your tap water, it will show up as "ash"—a chalky, white, harmless substance—on the surface of your soap. You can avoid ash by using purified water.

- **Lye** (aka Sodium Hydroxide)—Red Devil Lye is the most readily available and comes in convenient plastic containers with safety lids. Find it near drain cleaners in grocery and hardware stores. Don't buy Drano, or other drain cleaners, as they contain materials that will not work in soapmaking and could be dangerous to your health if used instead of pure lye. Shake each container before purchasing. Be sure it sounds like sand, not like rocks. If the lye is clumpy, you'll have to break it up prior to mixing with water.

Always wear rubber gloves and eye protection when handling lye, the lye solutions and infusions, raw soap mixture, and newly unmolded soap. Be sure to store lye containers out of reach of children, pet and others who may not understand its potentially hazardous nature. Be sure to have the numbers for the local poison control center and emergency room close at hand. You will most likely never need them, but it is good sense to have them where you can find them.

Additives

The recipes in this book are but a minuscule example of ways to enhance basic soap. Use the recipes as a starting place for your own creativity. You will find your creative juices really flowing as you get more and more into soapmaking. You'll want to make soap all the time, and when you're not making soap, you'll be thinking about it.

Additives

There are endless variations of what you can add to your soap. Choose your materials according to your magickal intent. You may make correspondences based on your particular tradition, astrological information, moon position, crystal and color vibration—anything you can devise to aid your intention. Your magickal recipe can be as general or specific as you like. Some examples: place Energizer soap in all the soap dishes in your house for daily use; reserve Full

Moon soap for those special Esbats. Your use of additives can also be as simple or complex as you like. You may, of course, make plain magick soap, infused with your intention only. Sometimes you may want a soap loaded with just the right essential oils, herbs, and spices for a specific spell. Just as often, the single soothing note of "your" essential oil is exactly what you want.

The following lists of essential oils, herbs, flower, spices, grains, resins, and other items cover the additives for the recipes in Part Two. Use the correspondences as a starting place, as a catalyst, for your own creative and magickal ideas. Be sure to keep track of the additives you need to get (or would like to try) on the Ingredient Shopping List in Appendix B.

Essential Oils

Choose pure essential oils according to your scent preferences and magickal correspondences. The recipes presented here use only essential oils.

 If you want a specific scent that isn't available as an essential oil, and magickal effect is unnecessary, by all means use fragrance oils. Know that synthetic scenting materials have no plant energy. Be sure to use fragrances that do not contain alcohol, as it will interfere with the chemical process. Perfume, cologne, and eau de toilette all contain alcohol. See Appendix E resources for soap-safe fragrance oils.

Store your essential oils in a cool, dark place in dark glass bottles. Treat them as you would all your magickal oils. The following list includes those oils employed in the recipes in this book but is by no means a comprehensive list. There is a vast array of wonderful books on essential oils and aroma-therapy, so you can learn as much as you like. If you can't locate a specific oil, or if an oil smells "wrong" to you, substitute with one that suits your magickal intention.

Scented geranium leaves

This table gives the common name of the plant from which the essential oil is derived, as well as the Latin name. Oils from many species and varieties are useful in soap. The species I've given are those I've found to be most common. For further information about essential oils, please consult an aromatherapy text, such as *Aromatherapy for Vibrant Health and Beauty: A Complete Guide to Understanding & Using* (Avery Publishing Group, 1995), by Roberta Wilson.

Essential oils are potent natural substances. Used incorrectly, they can cause adverse reactions. If you are extremely sensitive, be aware that even if used correctly, essential oils may irritate your skin. It's always best to err on the side of caution. If you are pregnant, nursing, or have special medical issues, including diabetes and epilepsy, please check with your healthcare practitioner before using essential oils.

Essential Oil	Properties
Cedarwood *Juniperus virginiana*	Strength, courage, rites of passage.
Chamomile *Anthemis nobilis*	Soothing, calming.
Clary Sage *Salvia sclarea*	Feminine energy, estrogen balancer. Promotes clarity of intention.
Geranium, Scented (or Rose Geranium) *Pelargonium graveolens*	Balance, feminine energy. Uplifting, helps create joy.
Jasmine *Jasminum officinale*	Full Moon energy. Happiness, relaxation, and love.
Lavender *Lavendula officinalis Lavendula vera,* etc.	Calming, cleansing, sleep-inducing. Antibacterial, antimicrobial.
Lemon *Citrus limon*	Feminine luminescence. Waning Moon energy. Strengthens resolve.
Oakmoss *Evernia prunastri*	Masculine energy, soothing, encouraging. Helps with meditative breathing.
Orange *Citrus sinensis*	Sun energy, potential, richness of life. Creates environment for a happy mood.
Patchouli *Pogostemon cablin*	Transport to the Otherworld. Opens the mind and psyche.
Peppermint *Mentha piperita*	Enlivening, strengthening, lifting. Clears breath.

Essential Oil	Properties
Pine *Pinus sylvestris*	Strength, warmth, constancy. Helps with meditative breathing.
Rose *Rosa damascena*	Love, peace, happiness. Romantic love, joy, and relaxation.
Rosemary *Rosemarinus officinalis*	Wisdom, self-esteem, protection. Heartening, calming.
Tea Tree *Melaleuca alternifolia*	Deeply cleansing, centering, affirming. Broad spectrum disinfectant.
Vetivert *Andropogon muricatus*	Deeply calming. Earth Mother energy.
Ylang Ylang *Cananga odorata*	Decorates and perfumes the beds of Indonesian newlyweds. Lifts spirits, reduces anger.

Lavender

There are many species of lavender, and "boutique" lavender essential oils from small growers are becoming more and more available. Even small lavender farms are producing varietal oils and specialized blends. If there is a lavender farm in your area, or if you travel to an area that is becoming known for growing lavender, be sure to visit and sample some of their oils.

For making soap, any kind of lavender essential oil will work well. I suggest saving the most expensive oils for applications other than soapmaking as lye is not kind to essential oils.

Herbs

If you have your own magickal garden, use herbs you've harvested. It is not difficult to grow them for magickal and culinary use—two of the easiest are basil and peppermint. From an elaborate garden to a few pots in the kitchen window, using herbs you've grown yourself creates another layer of energy in your magickal workings. If you have access to fresh herbs, dry them prior to incorporating them into soap. Even if you don't grow your own, there are many fine sources of magickal herbs, and the culinary herbs in your kitchen spice cabinet may also be dedicated to magickal purpose.

Herb	Properties
Basil *Ocymum basilium*	Sacred Masculinity. Dispels sadness.
Borage *Borago officinalis*	Courage, safe journeys. Happiness.
Comfrey *Symphytum officinale*	Soothing, comforting, encouraging.
Dandelion *Taraxacum officinale*	Reduces fear. Useful in manifesting intention.
Mugwort *Artemisia vulgaris*	Invokes the Moon. Feminine Divine. Protection.
Patchouli *Pogostemon patchouli*	Connects us to the Otherworld. Grounding, helpful in meditation.
Peppermint *Mentha pipeirta*	Enlivens, strengthens, brings courage. Helps us find renewal.
Rosemary *Rosemary officinalis*	Common sense, wisdom, protection. Encourages positive dreamstate.
Saffron *Crocus sativus*	Richness, bounty, renewal. Clothes one in Divinity.
Sage *Salvia vulgaris*	Ceremonial aroma. Lifts one beyond the mundane.
Yarrow *Achillea millefolium*	Healing, courage, forward motion. Divination.

In my soap room, I have a pole suspended from the ceiling from which I hang herbs to dry. You can do this in a dry place in your home, away from direct sunlight. A fast way to dry herbs is to lay them out on a cookie sheet overnight in the oven with just the pilot light on. If you have an electric range, heat the oven to 200 degrees, turn it off, and put the cookie sheet in overnight with the door open.

Many people believe that exposing any plant material to microwaves destroys any energetic properties. But you can, if it seems right to you, dry herbs in your microwave oven. Lay the fresh herbs in a single layer on a paper towel. Cover with three paper towels and microwave on high for two minutes. Check the herbs and repeat if necessary.

Whichever method you use, harvest and dry four Tablespoons of fresh herb to get one Tablespoon of dried herb. Some herbs, such as chamomile, are available in tea bags.

Close view of yarrow

34

Flowers

It's wonderful if you grow your own flowers—lavender and calendula are quite easy to tend—but it isn't necessary. If you do use flowers you've harvested from your magickal garden or gathered fresh, set them out to dry before incorporating them into your soap.

Flower	Properties
Calendula (or Pot Marigold) *Calendula officinalis*	Gentle and soothing. Place petals and oil in sun to make Calendula oil, which is very healing.
Chamomile *Anthemis nobilis* *Matricaria chamomilla*	Sedative properties. Use as a tea. Grind flowers for a gentle scrub.
Elder flowers *Sambucus canadensis*	Blessings, luck, fulfillment of wishes. Calms irritability.
Lavender *Lavandula vera, L. officinalis*	Sleep-inducing, soothing, grind for visual texture.
Rose petals *Rosa damascena or centifolia*	Imparts love and romance. Pink infusion fades in soap.

Close up of calendula and lavender flowers

 Many lavender farms have gift shops where you can buy dried lavender. And if you're there during cutting season, there is nothing like walking through a field of lavender and cutting your own.

Spices

Using ground spices in your soap can add color and texture. Most ground spices will feel a little scratchy, so if you don't like that feel, use in very small amounts, or use something else. Most of the following spices are available in powdered form. Use your mortar and pestle to grind those you purchase whole.

Spice	Properties
Annatto "seed" *Bixa orellana*	Sun energy. Dried pellets of pulp of the fruit. Grind as needed. Colors soap in warm tones from yellow to orange.
Black pepper *Piper nigrum*	Courage. Berry of pepper tree. Purchase ground rather than whole.
Cinnamon *Cinnamomum zeylanicum*	Warmth, home, and family. Purchase ground cinnamon for use in soap.
Cloves *Eugenia caryophyllata*	Warmth, love, home. Dried flower buds. Buy already powdered.
Nutmeg *Myristica fragrans*	Home, family. Gently strong masculine energy Dried seed. Grate whole nutmeg if needed.
Tumeric *Curcuma longa*	Masculine, solar energy. Imparts a yellow color to soap.

Grains

Grains and nuts add harvest energy to your magickal work. Be careful when using these additives, as they can be rough on the skin if you scrub too vigorously.

Grain	Properties
Cornmeal *Zea mays*	Masculine energy, Fertility.
Oatmeal *Avena sativa*	Water, Harvest energy, Ceres. Grind in coffee grinder to pulverize. Soothes the skin and has antiinflammatory properties.

Resins

Prized for the ability to open the mind to the Inner Spirit, resins have long been used in rituals. A base for incense, resins have a textural quality in soap. They also contribute to hardness and help the staying power of essential oils. Buy the following resins in powder form, or grind them in your mortar and pestle.

Resin	Properties
Benzoin *Benzoin styrax*	Traditional incense. Calming, centering, and encouraging.
Frankincense *Boswellia carteri*	Long used as sacred incense. Calming, helps with meditative breathing.
Myrrh *Commiphora myrrha*	Overcoming sorrow and adversity. Historical incense. Invokes refuge. Helps in finding your voice.

Other Items From Your Kitchen

Item	Properties
Coffee *Coffea arabica*	Feminine energy, yonic symbol. Espresso grind releases the most color.
Honey	Feminine energy. Antibacterial and humectant. Use in small amounts, as it can make soap overheat.
Maple Syrup	Use in small amounts, too much will get sticky. Masculine energy. Represents sweetness and the ability to "stick to it."

Colorants

There are many options available to you if you wish to add color to your magickal soap. These recipes use only botanical sources for color. Please note that when you use your soap, the natural colorants may still be potent. It will not affect your skin, but could possibly stain your wash cloths.

Color Magick is a study unto itself, and using color in your magick soaps will add more energy to your work. Lye is not kind to natural dyes from plants, but there are a few that will survive the chemical reactions and provide some color. Annatto seed, for instance, steeped in hot water will make a bright orange infusion that will lend a pretty orange color to your soap. Peppermint leaf, although bright green in the lye infusion, will fade to a faint green.

If you like, you can try regular food colorings to tint your soaps. Limit use to a few drops so you don't upset the balance of water and oils. Food colors behave unpredictably in cold-process soap. Blue and green may come out purple or mauve. Experimentation is the only way to know what will happen, as far as colors are concerned. It's all part of the magick!

Summary

Your options for adding wonderful things to your magickal soap are limited only by your imagination. To select particular additives based on their properties, consult the Table of Correspondences in Appendix C. You can always find something interesting to support your magickal intent. However, making unadorned soap can be just as powerful as making one loaded with magickal correspondences. As with any magickal practice, it's all about intent and personal energy.

I suggest choosing ingredients that are kind to the Mother. Even the most Earth-aware person has some impact on the planet, but doing what you can to investigate safe ingredients is a step in the right direction.

This book takes a Kitchen Witch's approach, employing an eclectic mix of correspondences. If you are on a particular path, apply what you have acquired from your workings about the way herbs, oils, plants, and colors work for you. If you are seeking a path, perhaps you'll find some inspiration through working with soap. Always experiment, always grow.

Sabbat soap bars

Chapter 2

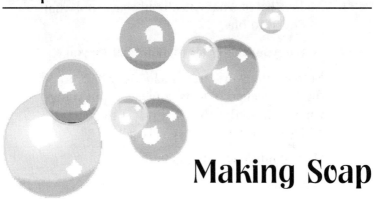

Making Soap

This chapter will take your through the actual "how to" of making your own magickal soap. Take your time to read and understand what to do before you dive in. Skim the chapter first, but it is essential that you read the whole thing, in detail, to be sure you get all the steps. Soapmaking is a process that involves many steps and usually takes a few trips to the store to get ready to go. The more time you spend in preparation, the easier and less stressful your first batches will be.

Getting Started

Please know that before actually doing it, making soap appears to be daunting. Worries about using lye safely, wondering if you're following the recipe accurately, concern about whether the reaction is happening yet are things all first-time soapmakers have experienced. Here are some tips:

- Read all instructions completely a number of times.

- Make a list of what you already have and what you need to buy.

- Get all your materials together before you start.

- Prepare the work area, including where to put the lye-touched objects, a place to put things you've finished with, etc. Protect the work surface and floor with newspapers.

- Have confidence in yourself.

- Have fun.

Why should I make my own soap?
Making your own soap has many benefits. The most important one is that you have total control over what you put in it. Many commercial soaps contain animal fats, petroleum products, preservatives, and other things you may want to avoid. Also, when you make your own soap, you can infuse it from the start with your own special magick.

Overview of the Steps

The Reaction

What makes soap? Without being too technical, soap is the product of a chemical reaction between a strong alkali and a fatty acid. In our case, *sodium hydroxide*—lye—and vegetable oils. This reaction is called *saponification*. The oils and lye solution combine in a vigorous reaction that creates soap and glycerin. You start the reaction when you combine the two in your soap pot (in this book, your 4-cup glass measure). The reaction continues after you've poured the soap into the molds. Once poured, the soap will heat up on it's own and after a short time will become translucent. As it cools, it will firm up and become opaque once again. Especially with small batches like the ones presented here, insulation of the molds is essential to be sure there is enough heat generated to go through those stages. That is why you wrap the soap molds with towels after you've poured it. As the soap ages, it becomes milder and milder as more and more of the ingredients react. Completely cured soap contains no active lye. The longer your soap ages, the more water evaporates, leaving the bar harder. You can use your soap four weeks after pouring, but the longer you wait, the longer the soap will last.

How Will I Know When the Reaction is Happening?

When you've combined the oils and lye solution, you will keep the mixture in constant gentle motion as the saponification begins. You'll notice a gradual change from translucent to opaque. There is also a very subtle yet unmistakable scent that will be released when the reaction really gets going. Perhaps you won't notice it right away, but after a few batches, you'll be reassured as you smell that familiar "soap" scent.

Trace

There are stages at which the soap mixture is ready for additives and then for pouring. These stages can be jointly referred to as "trace." Simply, trace means that if you take up a bit of the mixture on your spoon and drizzle it back onto the surface, it will stand for a bit before sinking back into the rest. "Is my soap tracing yet?" is probably the biggest source of worry for beginning soapmakers. Look for opacity and a tiny bit of graininess. I've often described the trace state as looking a bit like pancake batter. The more batches you make, the less stress you'll have over trace.

There are several levels of trace. Thin trace, medium trace, and full trace are the levels we'll work with.

Thin trace—soap drizzled on the surface makes little lines, and sinks back in almost immediately. This is a good stage for adding essential oils. Since the mixture is thin, the essential oils will disperse easily. Also, there are some essential oils that accelerate trace, making the reaction speed up. If the soap is already thick and this happens, it will be more difficult to pour.

Medium trace—soap drizzled on the surface makes thicker lines and takes a little while to sink back in. This is a good time to add things that are small and need to be evenly distributed like herb powders and spices. The soap is still thin enough that the mixing is easy, but not so thin that the particles will sink.

Full trace—soap leaves a distinct lump on the surface that sinks in after a couple of seconds. This is when you add heavy additives like oatmeal, lavender flowers, cornmeal, etc. The soap is thick enough to suspend the ingredient and keep it from sinking to the bottom.

Seizing—If the soap gets hard and clumpy all of a sudden, that means it has seized. All you can do if that happens, without special rescue techniques is spread the soap into the mold and let it go through the insulation stages. It will most likely be fine to use, just not easy to pour. Avoid this stage by adding essential oils early and pouring before the soap gets too thick.

These are not hard and fast technical terms, and will vary from soapmaker to soapmaker. After a number of batches, you'll come up with your own way of recognizing and working with the various stages of saponification.

Pouring

After the soap has traced and you've put in the additives, you're ready to pour the soap into a mold. There are many things you can use as a soap mold. I suggest a plastic drawer organizer with flexible sides. Rubbermaid makes the one I like the best. Make sure the mold is heat-proof so that it won't melt during the insulation phase.

The more you make soap, the more things you'll begin to see as potential soap molds. The plastic container section in the grocery store will take on a whole new fascinating aspect. The best soap mold is heat-proof, plastic, and flexible. Don't use your best expensive storage ware for soap molds.

Pour the soap into the mold with the mold set on the insulation towel on your work surface. When you've poured it all, cover the surface of the soap with plastic wrap. If your mold has a lid, close the lid over the plastic. Wrap the mold in the old towel. I just fold it over and gently arrange the rest on top to provide insulation.

Molds covered with plastic wrap

Insulation Period

Let the soap sit in the mold, wrapped in the towel for 48 hours. It needs to be out of the way of daily activity where it won't be disturbed. You can put it on top of the fridge, on a work surface you've designated for soap or other crafts—anywhere it won't get chilled or knocked onto the floor. The soap will probably be firm enough to move in about an hour, but wait about eight hours to be sure.

 Kitty alert: Cats are curious and love warm things. I've often had to chase my cats away from warm soap molds. When I make huge batches in great big molds with heavy, secure covers, it isn't such a problem, but it's easy for Kitty to push the little molds to the floor.

Unmolding

After two days in the mold, your soap is ready to come out. To make this easy, put the mold into the freezer for an hour or so to firm it up enough to release easily. Put on your gloves and goggles. Take out the mold, put it on the work surface. Pull off and discard the plastic wrap. Gently pull away the sides from the soap. Turn it upside-down on plain paper on your work surface. Gently press the bottom of the mold until the soap releases. After removing the soap, put the mold into the sink, giving it a little douse of vinegar.

Soap right after unmolding

Cutting

Use a regular stainless steel table knife to cut your unmolded soap into bars. Chose a bar size that you like. If your athame is made of a non-reactive metal, you may use it. If you're not sure, don't chance damaging the surface of your magickal tool.

Shaping

Some of the recipes give a suggestion to form the soap into special shapes appropriate to the recipe. Wear your rubber gloves when working with newly cut soap. If you want a smoother surface than the heavy rubber gloves give, get thinner gloves with smooth fingers just for this purpose.

Forming newly cut soap by hand

Curing

Lay the soap bars on edge and turn them every other day so that they'll cure evenly. Keep them out of direct sunlight and away from dust. I have a paper-covered cookie sheet in the guest room with curing soap on it most of the time.

Be sure to put a note in the curing area for each batch. Many of these soaps look a great deal alike and it is easy to get them mixed up. Write down the information you've put in your Soap Grimoire. Include date created, recipe, and estimated cured date.

Using

When four weeks have passed after you've poured your soap—what seems like an interminable wait—indulge yourself with a nice bath or long shower. Observe the way the soap feels, how it bubbles, and how it smells. After you've experienced the joy of using your soap, be sure to write down all your observations in your Soap Grimoire. All of your note-keeping will pay off as you make more and more soap.

Don't let your soap sit in water in the shower or tub—let it dry between uses. Since you've added neither artificial hardeners nor extracted the natural glycerin, your handmade soap will dissolve rapidly if left in a puddle. If a bar does escape and sits at the bottom of the tub for awhile, remove it and let it dry. It should firm up in a few days.

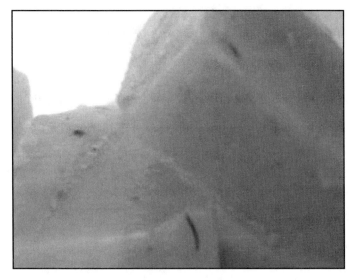

Close up on corner of soap bar

Loofahs, natural sea sponges, squares of linen fabric, and cotton terry are all excellent compliments to your soap. You can make pretty soap dishes that drain well using a glass or ceramic soap dish and partially filling it with marbles, stones, or beach glass.

Store cured soap in a cool, ventilated, dry place. Don't seal it in plastic containers. I like to keep a few bars in my sock drawer—they keep well there and work as a sachet. Another good place to store your magickal soap is in a box with your altar supplies.

Sharing

One of the most wonderful things in soapmaking is sharing what you've created. A handmade gift of such breadth as your magickal soap is a fantastic gift indeed. Be prepared for many requests! Suggestions for extending the creativity and magick through gift packaging can be found in Chapter 10.

 Don't let your friends hoard the soap gifts you give to them. "Too pretty to use" is not an acceptable phrase! Promise to make more soap for them, or even better, teach them how!

The Procedure

Now that you've gone through the overall "how to," let's get down to specifics.

The Basic Recipe

All the recipes in this book begin with one particular base. I strongly suggest making a plain batch first to get the feel of the procedure and of beautiful, basic soap. It will be referred to as the Basic Recipe.

When formulating this recipe, I took into account a number of factors. I wanted the ingredients to be easily available and affordable. I chose stable, predictable oils, with benefits for both soap and skin care. Olive oil makes a moisturizing soap with a low, stable foam. Coconut adds lathering and cleansing, however, too much can be drying. Castor oil acts as a lather booster, scent fixative, lubricant and "superfatting" agent. Superfatting means that there are extra oils in the soap after saponification. This ensures mildness and a moisturizing quality. If you decide to learn more about soapmaking and formulate your own recipes, you will discover a whole world of fascinating, and magickal possibilities. (There is a recipe in Appendix D for a pure olive oil soap.)

In all soapmaking, you must measure exactly. Especially in small-batch soapmaking like this, the proper ratio of lye to oil is essential. Using ingredients in such small amounts makes precision even more important—*you can't be even a little bit off.* The best way to measure ingredients for soap is by weight, so you need a good scale. An electronic postage scale and a kitchen scale that measures in .25-ounce increments, for example, are both good choices.

Basic Recipe

Lye Solution:

  2.5 oz. lye
  6 oz.   water

Oil Mixture:

    7 oz.   coconut oil
    10 oz.   olive oil

Additive:

    1 Tbs.   castor oil

1. Make a list and go shopping. A trip to a big grocery and a medium-sized health food store should take care of everything. Be sure to search your kitchen and your magickal supplies for something you already own. If you have limited access in your area, the Internet is the way to go. You can get supplies in small amounts from across the country in mere days. There is an ever-growing number of small distributors catering to the hobbyist soapmaker. There are some wonderful resources listed in Appendix E.

2. Copy down the recipe and procedures on a separate piece of paper, as it will most likely get ingredients on it as you work. Keep your Soap Grimoire handy to keep track of inspirations, or use scratch paper as you work, so you don't mess up your book too much. (I do, however, take pleasure in the essential oil spills and herb crumbs in the pages of my Soap Grimoire.)

3. Prepare the work area. Cover the work surface and floor with newspapers. Remember that you're not preparing the kitchen for a free-for-all disaster spree, so you don't need to surgically seal off everything. Just use common sense. Keep the vinegar close at hand.

4. Gather all ingredients and equipment.

5. Double check that you have everything you need. Having your soap ready to pour is not the time to realize you've forgotten something. Put on your gloves and goggles. There is no way to overemphasize the importance of this safety measure.

6. Measure exactly when making soap. Be sure your scale is accurate, and be sure to set it back to zero when you need to. Accuracy in soapmaking, especially in such small batches, is vital.

7. Place one of the Pyrex 4-cup measures on the scale. Set the scale to zero. Measure out 6 ounces of water. Some recipes in this book call for previously prepared infusions of herbs and water. Follow the directions for preparation in each recipe, and if necessary, measure out the infusion instead of plain water.

Infusions

8. Place a clean, dry, disposable plastic cup, such as you find in boxes of laundry detergent or a disposable drinking cup, on the scale. Set the scale to zero. Measure the lye into the cup. Put the cover back on the lye container and put it away.

9. Sprinkle the lye onto the water, stirring with a silicone spatula or wooden spoon. This solution will immediately heat up to almost boiling. Do not breathe the steam, as it is caustic. Stir gently, being careful not to splash, until the lye is dissolved completely. This should happen quite fast. When the lye is dissolved into the water, let the solution stand until it cools to 100 degrees. Some of the recipes call for an herb, spice or other additive to be infused in the lye solution. In this case, sprinkle the additive into the water *before* you add the lye.

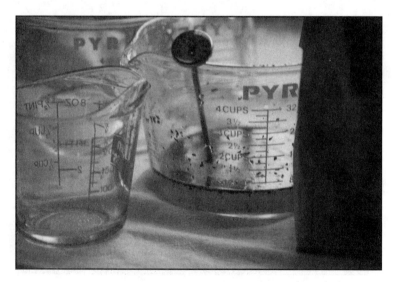

Peppermint lye infusion

10. While waiting for the lye to cool, combine the oils into the other Pyrex 4-cup measure.

 • Coconut oil is solid at room temperature. It begins to liquefy at about 80 degrees. If your coconut oil is solid, place the jar, uncovered, in a bowl filled with hot water. It should melt in a few minutes. You can measure out the olive oil while you're waiting.

 • Place the other 4-cup measure on the scale. Set the scale to zero. Pour in 10 ounces of olive oil.

 • Set the scale to zero, and pour 7 ounces of melted coconut oil into the olive oil. To avoid measuring mistakes, it's a good idea to measure the coconut oil separately *before* adding.

Warming coconut oil to add to olive oil while lye solution cools to temperature

Check the temperature of the oil mixture. You want it to be 100 degrees. To heat, put it into the microwave for 10 seconds on high. Stir and check the temperature. Do this until it is at 100 degrees. Be careful not to overheat, as it takes a long time for oils to cool.

11. When the lye solution and the oil mixture are both at 100 degrees, you are ready to combine them. With goggles and gloves on, slowly pour the lye solution in a fine stream into the oils. Stir with the other spatula as you pour.

Oils and lye infusion coming to temperature

When all the lye solution has been poured into the oils, place that Pyrex cup in the sink, fill it carefully with water and add about ¼ cup of vinegar. Let it sit in the sink while you work. When you've finished with other lye-touched objects, you can put them in this vinegar and water bath, too.

Closer view of lye solution just combined

12. Go back, right away, to the combined oil/lye solution. It's now time to stir. Depending on temperature of your work area, the humidity, etc. your soap should trace after 20 to 30 minutes of hand stirring. Watch and observe the reaction as you stir. It is quite a powerful experience. Ideas for magickal workings at this time are in Chapter 3.

Oils and lye solution just combined

13. Depending on the recipe you use, you'll make your additions at varying stages of trace.

Close view of opacity of traced soap

14. When all additions have been made, pour the raw soap mixture into the mold, cover with plastic wrap, place the lid over the plastic (if you have a lid), insulate with old towels, and put out of the way.

15. Clean up your work area. Wear your gloves and goggles while you clean up. Wash everything in warm water and dishwashing liquid, taking care not to splash, adding vinegar to anything that comes into contact with lye and raw soap. Don't rinse raw soap down the drain, as it will collect there, turn into soap, and clog your drain! Wipe out the soap cup before you wash it. Put all washable textiles in the washing machine with a little vinegar and the normal amount of laundry detergent.

16. Now, you wait. After the 48-hour period of insulation, chill the soap, unmold, cut it into bars, and set it away to cure and dry.

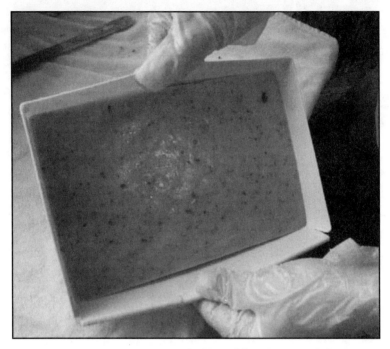

Unmolding Summer Solstice soap

If you are feeling overwhelmed at this point in reading, don't get discouraged. It seems like a lot, and it is, but it all makes sense when you do it. With practice, you'll be making batch after batch with ease. Over and over, talking with soapmakers through the years, we all mention the "addiction." Making soap is such a profound, powerful, and satisfying experience that once you're hooked, you can't get enough. Enjoy yourself. Take time to record your work. Relish the magick.

Cut bars

Chapter 3

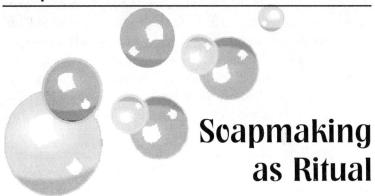

Soapmaking as Ritual

By now, you're probably wondering how this somewhat complicated process can be used as ritual. Or perhaps it's become clear to you just how much of a ritual it is. What follows are some ways to do soapmaking as ritual. Please use your own traditions, tools, ritual practices, and intentions in your discovery of this magickal process.

Like many Witches, my kitchen is a sacred space. I will often cast a Circle for special work, but for daily magick, the Circle is always in place. Whether or not I cast a Circle prior to making soap depends on how I feel, what the purpose of the soap is, and what has been happening in my kitchen recently. If there has been a big party with lots of unfamiliar energy around, I'll clear the space and reinforce the always-present Circle. For very special soaps, for Sabbats, Esbats, and Moon work for instance, I'll cast a Circle with the appropriate intention.

Calling the Corners

The Elements of Air, Fire, Water, and Earth are present in soapmaking. When I've measured the ingredients, sometimes I'll arrange them in their appropriate places on the work surface, corresponding to their appropriate places on the altar. When I make Moon soap at night, I have more freedom to spread out as the other members of the household are asleep. If you work at night, it is polite to have the clanking and banging part of your soapmaking done before everyone else retires.

I find that doing magick in a new way often requires a sense of humor as much as anything else. For example, if you've always been solitary, working with a group for the first time can be a source of unintentional hilarity. When a seasoned member of one tradition works in a different way than a guest or new member, all kinds of running into one another and missed cues abound. The same thing goes for these new workings. If finding yourself in your moonlit kitchen, suited up in your goggles, rubber gloves, and long sleeves, waving your wooden spoon about as you cast your first soap Circle doesn't inspire a fit of the giggles, I don't know what will. And that's to say nothing of your roommate wandering in for a night-time glass of water and finding you in full Magickal Soapmaking splendor. Mirth is part of the magick. Enjoy it. Just collect yourself and keep working.

These are some suggested correspondences for ingredient categories. Each ingredient has its own set of correspondences. Assign ingredients to Directions as they make sense to you. As you work, you will find that they are not always the same, and will vary with the intention. You will certainly find your own systems as you develop your Magickal Soapmaking skills.

Element	Direction	Ingredient
Air	East	Essential oils and other fragrance materials.
Fire	South	The lye solution, fire-related additives, castor oil.
Water	West	Water, coconut oil, olive oil, moon-oriented additives.
Earth	North	Resins, roots, grains.

A Sample Circle-casting

Center yourself. Use your mixing spoon as your wand as you ask the Elements for support and cast your Circle.

> *Elements of the East, I call on your energy to aid in this purpose. Fragrances are carried on your wind to lend their healing vibrations.*

> *Elements of the South, I call on your heat to be the catalyst for this transformative work. Base and acid combine to create this magickal substance.*

> *Elements of the West, I call on you to lend the power of the blood of the mother to be the cradle of this transformation, combining with you to bring magick to the mundane.*

> *Elements of the North, I call on your grounding energy to this work. Lend your focusing power to this process.*

Then make a prayer of intention. For example:

The mixing cup, my cauldron
the crucible of transformation.
The spoon, my wand
the agent of change.
The oils, the physical.
The lye, the energy
that blends and binds
the energies I've gathered and called
to this purpose.

Make the statement of your intention now. For example:

Whenever this soap will be used, love and light
will envelop whoever uses it.

Proceed with the mixing of lye solution and oils. Stir Sunwise, Moonwise, in circles, inscribing the pentacle, rune shapes, words, and other patterns according to purpose. This extended period of stirring is when you really charge the soap with your focused energy. It is easy to find a meditative and aware state during this time. Sing, chant, talk, or remain silent. Do what you need to do to focus the energy of your magickal intention on the chemical reaction brewing in your "cauldron."

 I really like the "She Changes" chant for this work. "She changes everything she touches and everything she touches changes." If you don't know this chant, see Starhawk's book, *The Spiral Dance*.

My favorite Rune for soapmaking is Laguz: ↑, the transformational, alchemical rune. Whatever work I'm doing, Laguz is always inscribed as I stir.

When you make your additions, take delight in how it recalls the Old Ways. I laugh when people ask about soapmaking and say, "So, it's sort of like 'eye of newt, toe of frog...?'" It is just like that. You are making something happen as you concentrate these energies into the highly charged reaction that is occurring in your soap "cauldron." Refocus yourself from your meditative state as you make the additions. You need to be fully present now. State the intention behind each addition as you make it and incorporate it thoroughly, perhaps making appropriate signs with your spoon as you do so. (Use common sense, of course—getting carried away with spoon- or wand-waving can splatter raw soap onto the ceiling—*not* a good thing.)

When you are ready to pour, focus your energy and will on your purpose as you move the raw soap from the crucible of transformation to the cradle of its rest and reaction. As you wrap the mold, finalize your spellwork.

Use the cleanup to dismiss and thank the Directions. Use Earth-friendly cleaning procedures such as using old towels instead of paper towels to wipe out the soap cup. Try to conserve water by pouring wash water from vessel to vessel. Be sure to use your vinegar to halt the reaction of any raw soap clinging to your tools.

Release the Circle and put everything away. Be sure to "ground" yourself with a bite to eat and a big glass of water before you lie down to rest and contemplate your magickal working—a sort of post-soapmaking Cakes and Ale.

PART TWO:

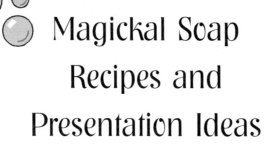

Magickal Soap Recipes and Presentation Ideas

The recipes in the following chapters include ritual elements with the ingredients and procedures. Use them as a starting place for your own creativity. If something doesn't make sense to you, by all means, change it. If something I've created works well for you as it is, that's wonderful.

Have fun, be creative, and be safe. I hope you enjoy making soap as much as I do. When you use your special creations on a daily basis or on holidays, you will know that your practice of Magickal Soapmaking brings magick into yet another facet of life.

In Chapter 10, you will find lots of suggestions for making your gifts of magickal soap even more special with creative wrappings and decorative accents. You'll learn what information you should provide with your soaps, as well as how to incorporate them into thoughtful and meaningful gift baskets for special occasions.

Chapter 4

Soapmaking
for Daily Living

Every day, we bathe. Whether in the shower or in the tub, we customarily start the day with a thorough cleansing. In the often stressful time of getting on with your day, it is easy to rush through your shower or bath giving little thought to the inherit sacredness. Even the busiest schedule has room for a deep inhalation and exhalation as you wash. When you're using your magickal soap, you'll partake of the magickal energy stored there. You'll find the soaps in this section helpful and luxurious for the daily and monthly cycles of your life.

The Energizer

Get a jump on your day. With the Energizer, you'll wake up and get ready to experience another series of miracles.

Orange essential oil is warm and enlivening. Oranges are a wonderful symbol of the sun and add outgoing energy. When you add it, call on the sun's energy to warm you to your day.

Peppermint is awakening and helps focus your mind. It is strong with masculine energy and tingles on the skin, making your body feel alive. As you make the infusion and add the essential oil, think of that tingly, alive feeling. Peppermint leaf will impart a very subtle green to the soap. The little green flecks will stay green for awhile and will eventually turn brown.

Black pepper contributes to courage and endurance. It offers protection and wards off danger. Add the pepper with a thought to safety and wellness.

Ingredients

Lye Infusion:

    2.5 oz. lye
    6 oz.   water
    ½ tsp. peppermint

Oil Mixture:

    7 oz.   coconut oil
    10 oz. olive oil

Additives:

    1½ tsp. peppermint essential oil
    1½ tsp. orange essential oil
    ⅛ tsp. black pepper, ground
    1 Tbs. castor oil

Procedure

Lye Infusion:

Add peppermint leaf to the water with the lye.

Blending:

- Make the lye infusion. Set aside to cool to 100 degrees.

- Combine the oils. Heat gently to 100 degrees.

- Slowly pour the lye infusion into the oil mixture when both are at 100 degrees.

- Add the peppermint and orange essential oils at light trace.

- Add the ground black pepper at medium trace.

- Add castor oil after everything else is added. Stir in well.

Stir to heavy trace, pour, and insulate as usual.

Lye solution mixed and ready to add peppermint leaf

Shape:

Cut into bars of substantial size, to encourage you to "get a grip" on your day!

The Relaxer

The Relaxer inspires us to breathe deeply and find rest. Sometimes we need to contemplate the day and let it go.

Chamomile and lavender are prized for their soothing, calming, and sleep-inducing properties. They are herbs for collecting your thoughts and letting them go so you can rest. If you are relaxed by a foot rub, leave the chamomile flowers coarse as they will make an excellent gentle scrub for the bottoms of your tired feet. Be sure to pick out any stems.

 Why is lavender in so many recipes? The name comes from the Latin *lavare*—"to wash." Lavender is the most amazing, wonderful plant. It is highly antimicrobial, antibacterial, and antiseptic. It is soothing to the mind, soul, and body. In fragrance, it blends well with almost any other essential oil.

Keeping a sachet of lavender flowers under your pillow will help you sleep. Laying stems of lavender in your dresser drawers imparts a lovely fragrance and protects against moths.

As you blend the ingredients for this soap, tell yourself a soothing bedtime story. Recall that story as you use the soap at the end of a long day.

Ingredients

Lye Infusion:

    2.5 oz.   lye
    6 oz.   water
    1 tsp.   chamomile flowers

Oil Mixture:

    7 oz.   coconut oil
    10 oz.   olive oil

Additives:

    1 Tbs.   lavender essential oil
    1 tsp.   lavender flowers
    1 Tbs.   castor oil

Traced soap, lavender ready to add

Procedure

Lye Infusion:

Add chamomile to the water with the lye. It will impart a light yellow color.

Blending:

- Make the lye infusion. Set aside to cool to 100 degrees.

- Combine the oils. Heat gently to 100 degrees.

- Slowly pour the lye infusion into the oil mixture when both are at 100 degrees.

- Add the lavender essential oil at light trace.

- Add the lavender flowers at medium trace.

- Add castor oil after everything else is added. Stir in well.

Stir to full trace, pour, and insulate as usual.

Shape:

After cutting into the desired size, shape the soaps into spheres, making a prayer for peace and rest as you form them.

Moontime

Moontime soap provides special care for the sacred woman's time. A soothing bath can help ease even the greatest of discomforts. You can also soothe your mate when she is menstruating with a tender bath.

Clary sage is a wonder of ancient and modern healing. It has been known through the ages as a soothing and centering oil—a great help in clarifying your thoughts. It is now known to be a great estrogen balancer.

Lavender soothes and lends gentle cleansing. Since some women are going back to the old way of using washable, reusable sanitary napkins, this soap is a great way to clean them. (See Appendix E for resources.) The lavender is a very good antibacterial agent and will help your pads stay fresh. After rinsing with cold water, squeeze out the water. Rub the soap onto the stain. Launder as usual.

Rose geranium, from the *Pelargonum* family of scented geraniums, is a potent oil for calming, soothing, and lifting the spirits. If you have a scented geranium plant, make some tea from the leaves. Sip this fragrant infusion and allow yourself to be soothed.

If you are a woman, make this soap while you are bleeding. If you no longer have your monthly courses, make it at a time that feels right to you. Also, make this soap with a young woman during her first courses.

Shaping Moontime soap

Ingredients

Lye Solution:
>   2.5 oz.   lye
>   6 oz.   water

Oil Mixture:
>   7 oz.   coconut oil
>   10 oz.   olive oil

Additives:
>   1 tsp.   clary sage essential oil
>   1 tsp.   lavender essential oil
>   1 tsp.   rose geranium essential oil
>   1 Tbs.   castor oil

Procedure

Blending:

- Make the lye solution. Set aside to cool to 100 degrees.

- Combine the oils. Heat gently to 100 degrees.

- Slowly pour the lye solution into the oil mixture when both are at 100 degrees.

- Add the clary sage, lavender, and geranium essential oils at light trace.

- Add castor oil after everything else is added. Stir in well.

Stir to full trace, pour, and insulate as usual.

Shape:

When you cut the soap, you can form the bars into spheres, then flatten into disks and mold into oval Yoni shapes. As you create the form, infuse the soap with soothing self-love and acceptance. The soap will be ready in a month, possibly for your next Moontime.

Chapter 5

Soapmaking for the Holidays

Creating special soaps for each holiday is a great way to focus your energy on the turns of the Great Wheel. Mentally and physically attuning to the changes in energy and intention, you can prepare for the seasonal observations with greater intent.

For your soap to be ready for the holiday, you need to make it a month in advance. A Samhian soap will be made at the end of September, Yule soap before Thanksgiving, and so on.

You don't have to use up each soap only through the holiday season, of course. Keep it and use its energy throughout the year. Better yet, share it with friends to spread the energy of the holiday.

Samhain—October 31

The Veil is thin during Samhain. This is the most magickal time of the year. It is a place between then, now, and future. It is a time for putting the past away and looking clearly into the possibilities of the future.

Patchouli herb and oil help you to access the place between the worlds. The smell is dark and rich, akin to the body of the Mother. The herb will darken the soap a little.

The coffee bean mimics the Yoni, the dark source of life. The ground bean darkens your soap to remind us of the darkness through which we must all pass.

Ingredients

Lye Infusion:

2.5 oz.	lye
6 oz.	water
½ tsp.	coffee, finely ground

Oil Mixture:

7 oz.	coconut oil
10 oz.	olive oil

Additive:

1 Tbs.	patchouli essential oil
⅛ tsp.	patchouli, ground
1 Tbs.	castor oil

Procedure

Lye Infusion:

Add Coffee to the water with the lye. It will get very dark and release a strong, mildly unpleasant odor. However, this odor will disappear.

Blending:

- Make the lye infusion. Set aside to cool to 100 degrees.

- Combine the oils. Heat gently to 100 degrees.

- Slowly pour the lye infusion into the oil mixture when both are at 100 degrees.

- Add the patchouli essential oil at light trace.

- Add the ground patchouli at medium trace.

- Add castor oil after everything else is added. Stir in well.

Stir to full trace, pour, and insulate as usual.

Shape:

Form soap into spheres. Decorate with whole coffee beans by pressing them into the surface of the soap when it is still soft. Make jack-o'-lantern faces, rune shapes, random patterns—whatever pleases you. As you work, infuse them with a sense of anticipation of the new year.

Shaping Samhain soap

Yule—Winter Solstice—Around December 21

Yule is a time of warmth and celebration, family time. It is also time to contemplate the deepness of the Dark Time. Many cultures have their stories of a "son of hope" born at the Winter Solstice. A shining star to brighten the lives of the people.

Cedar and pine are symbols of strength and wisdom. When feeling overwhelmed with the busyness and detail of the season, recall the strength of these symbols.

 Be sure when you buy essential oils made from trees that they are extracted from plantation sources and not old growth.

The power of clove is it's sweetness and it's ability to create harmony. As you add the clove, make a wish for a harmonious season.

Frankincense and myrrh, while readily available today, were once rare and prized as treasure. They have been used through the ages to connect us with the realm of Spirit. As you add the resins to your soap mixture, make a statement of intention to keep to the spiritual side of what can often be a very commercial and shallow time.

Ingredients

Lye Infusion:

    2.5 oz.   lye
    6 oz.   water
    ⅛ tsp.   clove, ground

Oil Mixture:

    7 oz.   coconut oil
    10 oz.   olive oil

Additives:

    1½ tsp. cedarwood essential oil
    1½ tsp. pine essential oil
    ¼ tsp. frankincense, ground
    ¼ tsp. myrrh, ground
    1 Tbs. castor oil

Procedure

Lye Infusion:

Add the clove powder to the water with the lye.

Blending:

- Make the lye infusion. Set aside to cool to 100 degrees.

- Combine the oils. Heat gently to 100 degrees.

- Slowly pour the lye infusion into the oil mixture when both are at 100 degrees.

- Add the cedarwood and pine essential oils at light trace.

- Add the frankincense and myrrh at medium trace.

- Add castor oil after everything else is added. Stir in well.

Stir to full trace, pour, and insulate as usual.

Shape:

When you cut the soap, form spheres and flatten them into disks. Inscribe a star—the pentagram—on them to recall the hope of the season.

Shaping
Yule soap

Imbolg—February 2

The first emergences occur around Imbolg. Crocus poke up through the snow. Woody herbs, such as rosemary, show new tender green leaves.

*Close view
of rosemary*

Like the groundhog, magickal people look around today and observe the weather. But, we don't have to wonder, we know spring is coming—the Eternal Return is just a little while away.

Saffron, the most precious of herbs, comes from the pollen stamens of the crocus. Even a few threads will infuse your soap with spring energy. If you don't want to use saffron, calendula petals are also very beautiful and full of the energy of the sun.

Rosemary—for remembrance, perhaps. Think about what remember means, if you break down the parts. *Re*member can be seen as the opposite of *dis*member. When you remember, you put all the parts back together. This is a wonderful image as you move from the darkness of winter into the potential of spring. Put all your disparate parts back together and get ready to grow.

Ingredients

Lye Solution:
> 2.5 oz. lye
> 6 oz. water

Oil Mixture:
> 7 oz. coconut oil
> 10 oz. olive oil

Additives:
> 1 Tbs. rosemary essential oil
> pinch saffron
> 1 Tbs. castor oil

Procedure

Blending:

- Make the lye solution. Seat aside to cool to 100 degrees.

- Combine the oils. Heat gently to 100 degrees.

- Slowly pour the lye solution into the oil mixture when both are at 100 degrees.

- Add the rosemary essential oil at light trace.

- Add the saffron threads at medium trace.

- Add castor oil after everything else is added. Stir in well.

Stir to full trace, pour, and insulate as usual.

Shape:

After cutting, shape into spheres and cut each one in half. Poke a hole through each hemisphere with a skewer. When the soap is cured, thread a length of yarn through the holes, reattaching the two halves.

Ostara—Vernal Equinox—Around March 21

Ostara is a time of rebirth and renewal. Bunnies and eggs represent a very old set of traditions. Nature is blooming with fertility. We can see the potentiality in everything, everywhere.

Peppermint and lavender are wonderful reminders of spring green and purple, aromatic beauties full of life and energy. Add them to your soap mixture with a thought of the growth and potential they represent. Don't be alarmed when the pretty green and purple of the fresh herbs turns to brown in the finished soap. It is just another reminder of the Cycle of Life.

Ingredients

Lye Infusion:

    2.5 oz.   lye
    6 oz.   water
    1 tsp.   peppermint

Oil Mixture:

    7 oz.   coconut oil
    10 oz.   olive oil

Additives:

1½ tsp. lavender essential oil
1½ tsp. peppermint essential oil
1 tsp.   lavender flowers
1 Tbs.   castor oil

Procedure

Lye Infusion:

Add peppermint to the water with the lye.

Blending:

- Make the lye infusion. Set aside to cool to 100 degrees.

- Combine the oils. Heat gently to 100 degrees.

- Slowly pour the lye infusion into the oil mixture when both are at 100 degrees.

- Add the lavender and peppermint essential oils at light trace.

- Add the lavender flowers at medium trace.

- Add castor oil after everything else is added. Stir in well.

Stir to full trace, pour, and insulate as usual.

Shape:

When you cut the bars, you can shape each one into egg shapes. After the soap has cured for a few days, inscribe runes or other magickal symbols with a toothpick.

Close view of peppermint leaves

Beltane—April 30, May 1

With the balance of male and female energy, Beltane is a time for coming together in a lovers' embrace. Yarrow for masculine energy balances the essential feminine of the rose.

Use a rose given as a gift for the rose petals in the soap. Recall the love and care with which it was given. If you have none saved, give yourself the gift of a single red rose and honor the love you have for yourself. Separate the petals, spread them out on a cookie sheet and let them dry out over night. They will lose their color and turn to brown specks in the finished soap, but they carry with them the love and intention of the rose at the height of its beauty. Think about what this means about the nature of love, and how it matures.

Ingredients

Lye Infusion:

    2.5 oz. lye
    6 oz.   water
    1 Tbs. yarrow, ground

Oil Mixture:

    7 oz.   coconut oil
    10 oz. olive oil

Additives:

    1 Tbs. geranium essential oil
    1 tsp.   red rose petals, dried
    1 Tbs. castor oil

Procedure

Lye Infusion:

Add yarrow to the water with the lye. It will add a light yellow color to the soap.

Blending:

- Make the lye infusion. Set aside to cool to 100 degrees.

- Combine the oils. Heat gently to 100 degrees.

- Slowly pour the lye infusion into the oil mixture when both are at 100 degrees.

- Add the geranium essential oil at light trace.

- Add the rose petals at medium trace. Crumble them onto the surface of the soap and stir in well.

- Add castor oil after everything else is added. Stir in well.

Stir to full trace, pour, and insulate as usual.

Shape:

After cutting, shape into Yoni and Lingam shapes. Press dried yarrow flowers and lavender flowers into the soap to decorate.

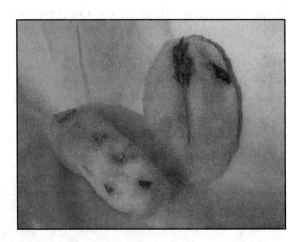

Beltane soap

Midsummer—Summer Solstice—Around June 21

Our Lady, at the height of her bounty, is ripe, full to bursting. At midsummer, we revel in the fruits of the season, and store away energy—physical, mental, and psychic—for the darkness that is coming.

Basil is an herb of the sun. The taste and smell of it recall the height of summer. It will fade to brown speckles in your soap, but knowing it's in there is like a ray of sun on your skin.

Benzoin is a reminder to never neglect the inner mind during this time of outward expression. The resin that helps fix the scent of orange can also help us fix on matters of spirit.

Orange is the essence of sunlight. Observe, as well, that it is the image of the rising Harvest Moon.

Annatto seed infusion makes this soap a bright, summery orange. If you can't find Annatto seeds, use turmeric instead. The color will be a light gold. Be careful of white washcloths—if the soap is left sitting on top, the cotton may pick up some of the natural dye.

Tracing soap mixture with herbs,
ready to add essential oils

Ingredients

Water Infusion:

6 oz.	water
1 Tbs.	annatto seeds (or substitute ½ tsp. ground turmeric)

Lye Solution:

2.5 oz.	lye
6 oz.	prepared water infusion

Oil Mixture:

7 oz.	coconut oil
10 oz.	olive oil

Additives:

1 Tbs.	orange essential oil
½ tsp.	benzoin resin
1 tsp.	basil, crushed
1 Tbs.	castor oil

Preparation

Water Infusion:

Make a strong infusion of water and annatto seeds by pouring six ounces of boiling water over one Tablespoon of the seeds. Let steep over night. Strain before adding lye. If evaporation has happened, add plain water to make the full six ounces. If substituting turmeric, use a half teaspoon to prepare the water infusion.

Procedure

Blending:

- Make the lye solution. Set aside to cool to 100 degrees.

- Combine the oils. Heat gently to 100 degrees.

- Slowly pour the lye solution into the oil mixture when both are at 100 degrees.

- Add the orange essential oil at light trace.

- Add the basil and benzoin at medium trace.

- Add castor oil after everything else is added. Stir in well.

Stir to full trace, pour, and insulate as usual.

Shape:

After cutting, shape the pieces into spheres and flatten them in to disks. Inscribe a solar cross on each disk.

Lammas—August 2

The feast of Lammas, also known as Lughnasadh, is a celebration of the first harvest. The fruits of our labors are coming in from the fields, metaphorically as well as literally.

When you're out in the sun, harvesting the bounty of your garden, or harvesting the fruits of your hard work on a vacation, be sure to take care of your skin. If you get too much sun, oatmeal soap can be very soothing.

Honey reminds us of the sweetness of work completed. It is a wonderful moisturizer and imparts a golden brown to your soap.

Ingredients

Lye Solution:
- 2.5 oz. lye
- 6 oz.   water

Oil Mixture:
- 7 oz.   coconut oil
- 10 oz.   olive oil

Additives:
- 1 Tbs.   oats, finely ground
- 1 Tbs.   honey
- 1 Tbs.   castor oil

Procedure

Blending:

- Make the lye solution. Set aside to cool to 100 degrees.

- Combine the oils. Heat gently to 100 degrees.

- Slowly pour the lye solution into the oil mixture when both are at 100 degrees.

- Add the oatmeal, basil, and benzoin at medium trace.

- Add castor oil and honey together, after everything else is added. Stir in well.

Stir to full trace, pour, and insulate as usual.

 Watch that the soap doesn't get too hot, as honey can add heat to the reaction. If the soap develops a crack in the center, take off the insulation.

Shape:

Shape the bars into loaf shapes, decorating with diagonal slashes.

Mabon—Fall Equinox—Around September 21

A time of thanksgiving and preparation as we look from the second harvest toward the Dark Time, Mabon can be the time to start final preparations for the new year, celebrated at Samhain. It is a time to take stock, make lists, and tie up loose ends. There are many kinds of harvests. As you make your lists, also keep track of what you're harvesting in your personal and spiritual life. Burn a little of the sage as you work, contemplating the bounty of your life.

Ingredients

Lye Infusion:

    2.5 oz.   lye
    6 oz.   water
    ½ tsp.   sage, ground

Oil Mixture:

7 oz.   coconut oil
10 oz.   olive oil

Additives:

1½ tsp. rosemary essential oil
1½ tsp. cedarwood essential oil
½ tsp.   myrrh resin, ground
1 Tbs.   castor oil

Procedure

Lye Infusion:

Add the ground sage to the water with the lye.

Blending:

- Make the lye infusion. Set aside to cool to 100 degrees.

- Combine the oils. Heat gently to 100 degrees.

- Slowly pour the lye infusion into the oil mixture when both are at 100 degrees.

- Add the rosemary and cedarwood essential oils at light trace.

- Add the ground myrrh at medium trace.

- Add castor oil after everything else is added. Stir in well.

Stir to full trace, pour, and insulate as usual.

Lye infusion and oils coming to temperature

Shape:

After cutting, shape the soap into crescents to symbolize the scythe, a universal symbol of harvest.

Chapter 6

Moon Phases

Keeping track of the phases of the Moon is one of the best ways to approach magickal awareness. She is always there, always changing. Planning by the Moon always gives you something to look forward to and helps you locate yourself in the cosmos.

Full Moon

Imagine the Moon, in her fullness, collected into something to hold in your hand. How lovely she is, on her ascent and descent. You can use this soap daily, filled as it is with her energy and your intentions. Or you can make it just to use when she is in her fullness.

Lemon is a beautiful symbol of the Moon and feminine energy. The scent of lemon blossom on the night breeze, the fragrant perfume of a freshly cut lemon is clean and full, rich with potential.

Mugwort is one of the strongest Water herbs. It grows on the banks of lakes and rivers, sending up strong stems to salute the Moon. It is intensely magickal, possessing properties ranging from helping you see the future to helping you to see deep inside yourself. The fresh leaves are silvery and soft, with downy white fibers running through the leaves. I like to think of these fibers as spun moonlight.

Benzoin resin is not just the base for sacred incense. It has a very practical use in soap. Citrus oils, like lemon and orange, can fade quickly. Benzoin acts as an anchor for fleeting citrus cents, as well as lending it's own sacred magick to the soap.

Ingredients

Water Infusion:
- 6 oz. water
- 1 tsp. mugwort, ground

Lye Solution:
- 2.5 oz. lye
- 6 oz. prepared water infusion

Oil Mixture:
- 7 oz. coconut oil
- 10 oz. olive oil

Additives:
- 1 Tbs. lemon essential oil
- 1 tsp. benzoin resin, ground
- 1 Tbs. castor oil

Preparation

Water Infusion:

On the first night of the Full Moon, place the ground mugwort in your cauldron or scrying bowl. Heat the water and pour it over the leaves, making an infusion. (Be sure your container can take the heat. If you are unsure, use one of the Pyrex 4-cup measures instead.) When it is cool enough to hold comfortably, take it outside. Settle yourself where you can see the Moon reflected in the surface of the water. Crumble some more mugwort leaves onto the surface of the water. Breathe in the steam and let your mind flow to the energy of the Moon. Look into the bowl and see. When you are finished, thank the Moon and take your container of mugwort and Moon infusion inside. You can make the soap now, or wait until day. When you prepare the lye solution, if some of the mugwort water has spilled or evaporated after making the infusion, replace it with fresh water to make a full six ounces.

Procedure

Blending:

- Make the lye solution. Set aside to cool to 100 degrees.

- Combine the oils. Heat gently to 100 degrees.

- Slowly pour the lye solution into the oil mixture when both are at 100 degrees.

- Add the patchouli essential oil at medium trace. This oil will probably darken the soap to a light brown.

- Add the ground frankincense resin at medium trace.

- Add castor oil after everything else is added. Stir in well.

Stir to full trace, pour, and insulate as usual.

Shape:

Shape into spheres, recalling the night you made the infusion. Press mugwort leaves into the soft soap, making designs that please you.

Dark Moon

In the monthly dark time, we gather ourselves inward. This is a time to begin a new project. As the Moon waxes to her fullness, our intentions come to fruition. Whatever goal you set for this Moon phase, using this soap and accessing the energy you've put into it will help you stay focused.

Patchouli and frankincense together make an incredibly strong magickal bond. This blend will help you to see forward and backward at the same time. Remember that making an intention isn't enough, you need to take the actions necessary to make your intentions manifest.

Ingredients

Water Infusion:

    6 oz.   water
    1 Tbs.   patchouli, ground

Lye Solution:

    2.5 oz. lye
    6 oz.   prepared water infusion

Oil Mixture:

7 oz.	coconut oil
10 oz.	olive oil

Additives:

1 Tbs.	patchouli essential oil
1 tsp.	frankincense, ground
1 Tbs.	castor oil

Preparation

Water Infusion:

On the first night of the Dark Moon, place the water and the patchouli herb in your scrying bowl or cauldron. Take it to your altar. Scry into the water, concentrating your intention, for the time, on going inward to stimulate growth. When you prepare the lye solution for your soap, if some of the patchouli water has spilled or evaporated after making the infusion, replace it with fresh water to make a full six ounces.

Procedure

Blending:

- Make the lye solution. Set aside to cool to 100 degrees.

- Combine the oils. Heat gently to 100 degrees.

- Slowly pour the lye solution into the oil mixture when both are at 100 degrees.

- Add the patchouli essential oil at medium trace. This oil will probably darken the soap to a light brown.

- Add the ground frankincense resin at medium trace.

- Add castor oil after everything else is added. Stir in well.

Stir to full trace, pour, and insulate as usual.

Shape:

After cutting, shape into spheres, concentrating on your intention as you form them.

Chapter 7

Soapmaking for Special Occasions

Handfasting

Two people coming together and deciding to make a commitment to each other in front of their community of family and friends is one of the most joyous occasions in life. Whether the couple pledges love for "a year and a day" or for eternity, it is a reason to celebrate.

Orange flowers have long been used in wedding bouquets. You can capture the essence by using orange flower water to make the lye solution. Roses are often given as a token of affection. Oakmoss is full of yin energy, and ylang ylang is full of yang energy, making an excellent complimentary bond.

One the of most important things that can happen during the ceremony is for those witnessing the union to pledge to help the couple as they move forward into their life together. Making enough soap to cut into favor-sized chunks to share with the guests is a wonderful way for them to continue this pledge. Wrap them in pretty paper with a tag attached explaining the spell. (And make sure your guests know it isn't cake!)

Ingredients

Lye Solution:
    2.5 oz. lye
    6 oz.   orange flower water

Oil Mixture:
    7 oz.   coconut oil
    10 oz.   olive oil

Additives:
    1 tsp.   ylang ylang essential oil
    1 tsp.   oakmoss essential oil
    1 tsp.   rose petals, finely ground
    1 Tbs.   castor oil

 Because oakmoss essential oil is extremely viscous and sticky, it will not disperse well in the soap mixture alone. Dissolve the oakmoss by stirring it together with the ylang ylang essential oil, making it easier to combine.

Procedure

Blending:

- Make the lye solution with the orange flower water. Set aside to cool to 100 degrees.

- Combine the oils. Heat gently to 100 degrees.

- Slowly pour the lye solution into the oil mixture when both are at 100 degrees.

- Add the essential oils at medium trace

- Add the ground rose petals at medium trace.

- Add castor oil after everything else is added. Stir in well.

Stir to full trace, pour, and insulate as usual.

Shape:

After cutting, shape the soap into disks. Cut an "S" shape down the center of the disk to make the yin and yang shapes.

Partially stirred, light trace

Lovemaking

The physical expression of love is one of most holy experiences adults can share. Preparing the mind and body for the ongoing act of making love is one of the most important parts of adult life. Honoring each other's bodies through ritual bathing is a great prelude to sexual expression.

Ylang Ylang has long been prized for its reputation as an aphrodisiac. Its sweet, heady aroma prepares the heart chakra for opening. Kundalini energy is coaxed through the root and out the crown by patchouli. Precious jasmine and rose absolutes are expensive, but they are unbelievably beautiful scents that deepen the heart connection. You can replace the water with rosewater, to add more of the love essence to your soap.

Ingredients

Water Infusion (optional):

6 oz.	water
1	fresh red rose

Lye Solution:

2.5 oz.	lye
6 oz.	water (or prepared rosewater)

Oil Mixture:

7 oz.	coconut oil
10 oz.	olive oil

Additives:

1 tsp.	scented geranium essential oil
1 tsp.	patchouli essential oil

1 tsp.	ylang ylang essential oil
10 drops	jasmine absolute
10 drops	rose absolute
1 Tbs.	castor oil

Preparation

Scented geranium flower

Water Infusion:

To prepare the rosewater, remove the fresh petals from one red rose and discard the stem. Place the petals in a bowl with six ounces of boiling water. Allow to steep overnight. Strain the petals from the infusion and use the resulting rosewater in place of regular water in the lye solution.

Making rose petal infusion

Procedure

Blending:

- Make the lye solution. Set aside to cool to 100 degrees.

- Combine the oils. Heat gently to 100 degrees.

- Slowly pour the lye solution into the oil mixture when both are at 100 degrees.

- Add the essential oils at medium trace.

- Add castor oil after everything else is added. Stir in well.

Stir to full trace, pour, and insulate as usual.

Shape:

After cutting, shape into heart shapes, imbuing the soaps with your hopes and dreams for joy in sexual union.

New Baby

Bringing a new life into the world is the most important thing we do as humans. Whether giving birth or adopting, preparing the house for a new baby is a grand occasion. Making this soap is a wonderful project for a baby shower.

Chamomile and lavender are very beneficial for baby. They both have soothing properties, and lavender is especially good as an antimicrobial. They are used in small amounts in this recipe for a gentle touch.

In some traditions, Wiccaning, the formal dedication of a child to the care of the Great Mother Goddess, is a joyous event for a magickal family. Spells of protection figure heavily when placing the child in the arms of the Goddess.

Each day, everyone in the family can recall the event by sharing the energy of a soap created just for this purpose.

 Remember, the soap should not be used on a newborn. Save the soap for babies 6 months and older, and be sure to rinse well.

Ingredients

Lye Solution:

    2.5 oz.   lye
    6 oz.   water

Oil Mixture:

    7 oz.   coconut oil
    10 oz.   olive oil

Additives:

½ tsp.   chamomile essential oil
½ tsp.   lavender essential oil
1 Tbs.   castor oil

Procedure

Blending:

- Make the lye solution. Set aside to cool to 100 degrees.

- Combine the oils. Heat gently to 100 degrees.

- Slowly pour the lye solution into the oil mixture when both are at 100 degrees.

- Add the chamomile and lavender essential oils at medium trace.

- Add castor oil after everything else is added. Stir in well.

Stir to full trace, pour, and insulate as usual.

Shape:

When the soap is ready to cut, instead of cutting, press the soap into a flat mass, about ½ inch thick. Be sure to wear your rubber gloves. Using a stainless steel knife, cut out into simple shapes like sheep, ducks, fish, etc. Use a stainless steel pancake turner to transfer the shapes to the curing area. If you prefer something more simple, you can form spheres, or flatten the spheres into disks with baby's initial carved in.

New Companion Animal

Bringing a new animal companion into the home is an extremely important event for anyone. For some magickal people, companion animals are also our familiars—our embodied companion spirits.

Whether a baby animal or a seasoned companion, any animal can make a mess when introduced to a new living situation. The tea tree oil in this soap that will help fight fleas as a dog shampoo is also good for treating and deodorizing stains on carpets and bedding. Be sure to test the fabric or carpet in an inconspicuous place before using on the stain.

Naughty Bunny

Make a prayer for patience and abiding love as you prepare this soap for you new loved one.

Ingredients

Lye Solution:

    2.5 oz. lye
    6 oz.   water

Oil Mixture:

    7 oz.   coconut oil
    10 oz. olive oil

Additives:

    1 Tbs. tea tree essential oil
    1 Tbs. castor oil

Procedure

Blending:

- Make the lye solution. Set aside to cool to 100 degrees.

- Combine the oils. Heat gently to 100 degrees.

- Slowly pour the lye solution into the oil mixture when both are at 100 degrees.

- Add the tea tree essential oil at medium trace.

- Add castor oil after everything else is added. Stir in well.

Stir to full trace, pour, and insulate as usual.

Shape:

Cut into blocks of a size that is easy to hang onto as you scrub your companion animal or the carpet.

Parting

Part of being civilized is breaking up in a reasonable way. Pain and hurt can be soothed through the comfort of community ritual.

Forgiveness is a great measure of parting. A good way to forgive is to symbolically wash away the slights, real and imagined. As you create this soap, infuse the soap with all the bad things you want to wash away. As you use the soap, visualize those things that hurt you going down the drain and being replaced by the soothing ingredients on your skin.

The poppy itself is a natural, soothing symbol. Poppy seeds serve as an exfoliant to help gently scrub away the past.

Ingredients

Water Infusion:

See instructions for lavender and chamomile tea in "Preparation" following the ingredients.

Lye Solution:

    2.5 oz.   lye
    6 oz.   prepared lavender and chamomile infusion

Oil Mixture:

    7 oz.   coconut oil
    10 oz.   olive oil

Additives:

    1 tsp.   poppy seeds
    1 Tbs.   castor oil

Preparation

Water Infusion:

As you talk with the person from whom you are parting, make a strong tea of lavender and chamomile flowers and set it on the table to steep. Leave the infusion on the table for a day, and every time you pass by, leave another hurt there. Or if it is your friends who are parting, have one or both friends over for a talk. Allow the tea to steep during the conversation, and incorporate it into your soap after they have gone. To use the infusion, strain out the herbs and add enough water to make six full ounces.

Procedure

Blending:

- Make the lye solution with the prepared infusion. Set aside to cool to 100 degrees.

- Combine the oils. Heat gently to 100 degrees.

- Slowly pour the lye solution into the oil mixture when both are at 100 degrees.

- Add the poppy seeds at medium trace. When you add the poppy seeds at medium trace, make a prayer for the sloughing of your hurt. (Be sure, when you use your soap, that the scrubbing is just symbolic—treat your skin gently.)

- Add castor oil after everything else is added. Stir in well.

Stir to full trace, pour, and insulate as usual.

Shape:

After cutting, shape into spheres. When they have firmed a bit, cut the spheres in half, keeping the two halves next to each other. When the soap is ready, give half of yours to your former partner and keep half for yourself, or give the halves to the people who have parted.

Hospice

One of the saddest parts of death in Western cultures is that many people die alone, without family to attend them. Experiencing the crossing over of a loved one is a beautiful experience for those fortunate enough to be with the loved one during this time. Hospice care can include comforting and caring for the person who is preparing to go. If this in-cludes the task of lovingly bathing your dear one, you can include this soap in the process.

Deciding when to make this soap can be an emotional experience. Having it "on hand" can seem pessimistic or morbid. Use the making of this soap to explore your feelings about death. Perhaps when you've had a dream about death, or when you decided to put together your will. Death is part of the Great Cycle, and with strength, we can come to peace with it.

Hecate is an aspect of the Goddess associated with guid-ing the dead on their journey. Patchouli is sacred to Her, as is vetiver. They are both are redolent with the smell of the Earth herself. Herbs associated with Hecate include dandelion and mint.

Ingredients

Water Infusion:

    6 oz.   water
    2 Tbs.   mint leaves
    2 Tbs.   dandelion leaves

Lye Solution:

    2.5 oz. lye
    6 oz.   prepared water infusion

Oil Mixture:

    7 oz.   coconut oil
    10 oz.   olive oil

Additives:

    2 tsp.   patchouli essential oil
    1 tsp.   vetiver essential oil
    1 Tbs.   castor oil

Preparation

Water Infusion:

The night before you make the soap, make a strong infusion of the dandelion and mint leaves with six ounces of boiling water. Scry into the solution as it cools. Contemplate the meaning of leaving this life and moving on. Put your prayers for safe and gentle crossing into the infusion.

Procedure

Blending:

- Make the lye solution with the infusion. Set aside to cool to 100 degrees.

- Combine the oils. Heat gently to 100 degrees.

- Slowly pour the lye solution into the oil mixture when both are at 100 degrees.

- Add the essential oils at medium trace.

- Add castor oil after everything else is added. Stir in well.

Stir to full trace, pour, and insulate as usual.

Shape:

After cutting, shape into bars that will be easy to hold.

Chapter 8

Soapmaking for Women

Menarche

One of the most important things we can do for our daughters is to welcome them to womanhood with love, care, and information. Welcome the young woman into the company of women with a gathering appropriate to the girl's nature. Some young women would relish a grand event with lots of aunties, friends, and grandmothers, where another would love to go shopping with her mother and maybe a close friend.

Whatever the girl wants to do to mark her special time, creating a soothing soap for her to use during her first Moon Time is a thoughtful gift. Clary sage and chamomile are both very soothing and are helpful in a warm bath to cleanse and soothe cramps.

Ingredients

Lye Solution:
2.5 oz.   lye
6 oz.   water

Oil Mixture:
7 oz.   coconut oil
10 oz.   olive oil

Additives:
1 Tbs.   clary sage essential oil
1 tsp.   chamomile, ground
1 Tbs.   castor oil

Procedure

Blending:

- Make the lye solution. Set aside to cool to 100 degrees.

- Combine the oils. Heat gently to 100 degrees.

- Slowly pour the lye solution into the oil mixture when both are at 100 degrees.

- Add the clary sage essential oil at medium trace.

- Add the ground chamomile at medium trace.

- Add castor oil after everything else is added. Stir in well.

Stir to full trace, pour, and insulate as usual.

Shape:

After cutting, shape into spheres. Roll the soft soap in the pretty chamomile flowers.

Motherhood

After the birth or adoption of a child, a woman is empowered and drained at the same time. So often we shower the newborn with our attention, even to the extent that we don't take into consideration the special care that a woman needs as she begins healing and adjusting to life with her new baby. One of the nicest gifts you can give to a new mother is a special, pampering soap, made especially with her needs in mind.

Chamomile is soothing to skin healing from the trauma of giving birth, vaginally or by caesarian section. Rose absolute is very expensive, but it embodies love in its fullest and is perfect for a new mom. Cinnamon symbolizes warmth and the comforts of home. Lavender is antibacterial and soothing as well.

Ingredients

Water Infusion:

    6 oz.   water
    ¼ cup   chamomile

Lye Solution:

    2.5 oz.   lye
    6 oz.   prepared water infusion

Oil Mixture:

7 oz.   coconut oil
10 oz.   olive oil

Additives:

10 drops   rose essential oil
tiny pinch   cinnamon, ground
1 Tbs.   castor oil

Preparation

Water Infusion:

The night before you make the soap, on the first night of the full moon, make a very strong infusion of chamomile using six ounces of boiling water and ¼ cup of chamomile. Carry the container outside to where you can see the moon reflected in the surface. Meditate on the fullness of motherhood, happiness for mother and baby, and abiding love. When the infusion cools, strain out the chamomile and compost it. When preparing to make the soap, if necessary, add fresh water for six full ounces to use in the lye solution.

Procedure

Blending:

- Make the lye solution with the infusion. Set aside to cool to 100 degrees.

- Combine the oils. Heat gently to 100 degrees.

- Slowly pour the lye solution into the oil mixture when both are at 100 degrees.

- Add the rose essential oil at medium trace.

- Add the ground cinnamon at medium trace.

- Add castor oil after everything else is added. Stir in well.

Stir to full trace, pour, and insulate as usual.

Shape:

After cutting, form into egg shapes to symbolize the fullness of the potential symbolized in the round belly.

Croning

Entering the postmenopausal age is a time of freedom and empowerment for most women. We are returning to an age in which the Crone is to be honored, revered, and respected rather than cast aside. Sometimes a younger woman goes through menopause early for a variety of reasons. No matter when a woman enters her Cronehood, she is deserving of a demonstration of respect for her special needs at this time, including a long, uninterrupted bath.

As with making soap for Menarche, ask the woman what she wants to do. Some women want to let out all the stops, having a huge party. Some women prefer a period of quiet introspection. Some women may want a combination of both. Making this soap can be a part of the celebration. Black cohosh can be very useful at cronehood, as is clary sage.

Ingredients

Water Infusion:

    6 oz.   water
    3 Tbs.   lavender flowers

Lye Solution:

2.5 oz. lye
6 oz. prepared water infusion

Oil Mixture:

7 oz. coconut oil
10 oz. olive oil

Additives:

1 Tbs. clary sage essential oil
1 tsp. black cohosh, ground
1 Tbs. castor oil

Preparation

Water Infusion:

The night before making the soap, make a strong infusion with six ounces of boiling water and three Tablespoons of dried lavender flowers. As the infusion cools, fill it with positive energy focused on the beauty of the maturing woman.

Procedure

Blending:

- Make the lye solution using the lavender infusion. Set aside to cool to 100 degrees.

- Combine the oils. Heat gently to 100 degrees.

- Slowly pour the lye solution into the oil mixture when both are at 100 degrees.

- Add the essential oil at medium trace. This oil will probably darken the soap to a light brown.

- Add the ground black cohosh at medium trace.

- Add castor oil after everything else is added. Stir in well.

Stir to full trace, pour, and insulate as usual.

Shape:

After cutting, shape into sphere, oval, and pear shapes, and other rounded forms to honor the shape of woman.

Chapter 9

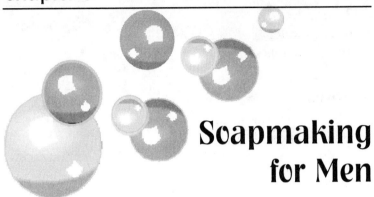

Soapmaking for Men

Quest

In many Western cultures, there are few formalized events to mark a young man's entry into society as a man. Whereas a girl enters womanhood through her Menarche, there is nothing as biologically clear for a boy. The rites of the Jewish bar mitzvah and the Native American vision quest can provide keys toward the creation of rituals to help our sons formalize the taking of their place in society as a man.

Look for stories of hero quests to share with the young man. Adventures involving overcoming fear, widening spirit boundaries, and taking responsibility are especially pertinent.

Yarrow is an herb of courage. Mythical Achilles used it to staunch the bleeding from his soldiers' wounds. Rosemary can help with common sense and self-assurance. Sage is used in many cultures to lift the spirit above the mundane world. Use a little maple syrup in the lye infusion to evoke long life and sweetness.

Ingredients

Lye Solution:

- 2.5 oz. lye
- 6 oz. water
- 1 tsp. maple syrup

Oil Mixture:

- 7 oz. coconut oil
- 10 oz. olive oil

Additives:

- 1 Tbs. rosemary essential oil
- 1 tsp. yarrow, ground
- 1 tsp. sage, ground
- 1 Tbs. castor oil

Grinding dried sage leaves using a mortar and pestle

Procedure

Blending:

- Make the maple syrup lye solution. Set aside to cool to 100 degrees.

- Combine the oils. Heat gently to 100 degrees.

- Slowly pour the lye solution into the oil mixture when both are at 100 degrees.

- Add the essential oil at medium trace. This oil will probably darken the soap to a light brown.

- Add the ground herbs at medium trace.

- Add castor oil after everything else is added. Stir in well.

Stir to full trace, pour, and insulate as usual.

Shape:

After cutting, shape into arrows, wands, and other symbols of masculine energy, concentrating on your intention as you form them.

Love-Partnership

A man entering a marriage, handfasting, life-partnership, or other form of public binding with another is a beautiful thing. Whether with a woman, or in a same-sex union, our grooms need to be treated with great love and attention.

Traditionally, a bride-to-be is showered with gifts for the home, while the groom-to-be is expected to participate in some kind of debauchery. Perhaps we can evolve beyond this division and have the couple and their friends celebrate the impending union together, honoring them in a more enlightened way.

Regardless of what way their friends will shower the couple, the groom-to-be can shower with soap carrying the best intentions of his community of friends.

Elder flowers offer blessings and fulfillment of wishes. Cedarwood essential oil adds the symbolism of strength and chamomile is for gentleness.

Ingredients

Lye Infusion:

    2.5 oz. lye
    6 oz.   water
    1 Tbs.   ground elder flowers

Oil Mixture:

    7 oz.   coconut oil
    10 oz.   olive oil

Additives:

    1 Tbs.   cedarwood essential oil
    1 tsp.   chamomile, ground
    1 Tbs.   castor oil

Procedure

Lye Infusion:

Combine the ground elder with the lye and water when you make the solution.

Blending:

- Make the lye infusion. Set aside to cool to 100 degrees.

- Combine the oils. Heat gently to 100 degrees.

- Slowly pour the lye infusion into the oil mixture when both are at 100 degrees.

- Add the essential oil at medium trace.

- Add the ground chamomile at medium trace.

- Add castor oil after everything else is added. Stir in well.

Stir to full trace, pour, and insulate as usual.

Shape:

After cutting, shape into spheres, to symbolize the Circle of Life, and cubes, to symbolize stability and centeredness. Concentrate on your intention as you form them.

*Grinding
chamomile*

Fatherhood

Becoming a father is the most important thing a man can do. Whether through birth given by his partner, adoption, or any of the other ways a man can become a father, honor must be given. A man needs love, courage, strength, and patience to be a father. In equal measure, he needs gentleness, creativity, and a sense of fun.

Borage is a tough-stemmed herb with great healing and soothing properties. Comfrey is healing and makes a wonderful charm for a safe journey. Oakmoss essential oil (a very thick resinous substance) and lavender essential oil combine for strength and gentleness.

Ingredients

Water Infusion:

6 oz.	water
1 Tbs.	borage
1 Tbs.	comfrey

Lye solution:

2.5 oz.	lye
6 oz.	prepared water infusion

Oil Mixture:

7 oz.	coconut oil
10 oz.	olive oil

Additives:

1 tsp.	oakmoss essential oil
2 tsp.	lavender essential oil
1 Tbs.	castor oil

Preparation

Water Infusion:

The night before making the soap, make an infusion using six ounces of boiling water with one Tablespoon each of borage and comfrey leaves. As the infusion steeps, make a prayer, chant, or other verbal expression of what makes a good father. Strain the infusion, compost the herbs. Use the infusion in your lye solution.

Procedure

Blending:

- Make the lye solution. Set aside to cool to 100 degrees.

- Combine the oils. Heat gently to 100 degrees.

- Slowly pour the lye solution into the oil mixture when both are at 100 degrees.

- Add the essential oil at medium trace. (Dissolve the thick oakmoss oil in the lavender oil so you can add it to the mixture easily.)

- Add castor oil after everything else is added. Stir in well.

Stir to full trace, pour, and insulate as usual.

Shape:

After cutting, shape into spheres, then flatten them into disks. Inscribe the initials of the father-to-be on them.

Chapter 10

The Presentation

So, what are you going to do with all this soap? One person, one household can only be so clean! Sharing your Magickal Soap creations is one of the best parts of this craft. When you get into the rhythm of making soap for the holidays, you will never be caught with nothing to give the hosts of the feast!

I have often found myself, on the way out of the house, grabbing a few bars off the curing rack and stuffing them into a resealable bag to take as a last minute gift. I've often wished I had some specially packaged bars on hand to take on the spur of the moment. So, with these suggestions and your own imagination, you can create wonderful gifts to take along!

Packaging for presentation can range from very simple to extravagant. Sometimes a simple length of twine or handmade yarn is just right. Sometimes you want to go all-out, extending the theme of the soap itself.

I like raffia and natural fiber yarns for tying. Mulberry and other decorative papers are wonderful. If you make your own paper, that would make an extra-special addition to your gift. Adding some of the herb used in the soap to the paper-pulp mixture would be beautiful!

If you want to put your soap in a bag, breathable fabric is better than plastic or cellophane. Some plastic and cellophane bags are very pretty and convenient, though. Just be sure to let some air into the bag, and let your friend know not to keep the soap air tight. Try cutting squares of decorative fabric to use as "wrapping paper." (Always pre-wash and thoroughly dry fabrics prior to wrapping soap.)

It is a good idea to make a card, which should include the ingredients, magickal working, and your thoughts and feelings

Soap bars cut in two different sizes

about your gift. Rubber stamps are available with Goddess and Pagan symbols. List the ingredients with their symbolic, magickal, and healing properties. Be sure you include the information that the soap needs to dry between uses and that it should be used within a few months, for best quality. You will find your handmade Magickal Soap a welcome and hoped for, if not outright requested gift!

These specific gifting ideas are just that—ideas upon which to build the "perfect" gift. After a few years, I thought that my friends and family were getting tired of soap, so I stopped giving it as gifts. I was pleased to find out that they missed getting it.

Occasions

Baby Gift

- New Baby and Motherhood soaps.

- Soft baby wash cloths.

- Chamomile, tied in fabric bundles, to use as "bath tea."

Make the bundles by cutting baby-themed cotton fabric in 4 x 4-inch squares with a pair of pinking shears. Place two to three tablespoons of chamomile flowers in the center of each fabric square. Gather up the edges, packing the chamomile a little. Close the bundle by wrapping thin ribbon tightly. Use square knots, and tie a decorative bow. Trim the ends.

Place the soaps, cloths, and chamomile bags in a decorative drawer organizer with holes for drainage, or a plastic basket. Either would be perfect, as it could corral all of these bathing items and allow them to drain.

Write the ingredients and magickal intent on the card, adding something like: "The herbs and essential oils in these soaps were carefully selected to soothe and care for you and baby. The little bundles of chamomile are to be used in the tub as a gentle bathing tea."

 Remember, the soap should not used on a new-born. Save the soap for babies 6 months and older, and be sure to rinse well.

Handfasting Basket

- Handfasting, Love-Partnership, and Lovemaking soaps.

- Luxurious washcloths in the lovers' favorite colors or handfasting theme colors.

- Scented votive candles in holders, color-coordinated with the washcloths.

Choose washcloths of the finest quality cotton. Make an attractive presentation by folding the cloths into rectangles and placing the soaps on top. Make a bundle by tying a pretty coordinating ribbon around the soap and cloth, centering the knot on the soap. Place the cloth and soap bundles side by side in a basket. Arrange the candles, in holders, on the sides.

Along with ingredients, instructions, and magickal intents of the soaps, write something like: "Bathe each other in love every day."

Friends in Deed

What is better than a visit from a good friend when you're going through a hard time? Visit a friend in need with a basket of treats that will pamper and soothe her.

- Soap appropriate to the situation.

- Large, natural sea sponge for rinsing and lathering.

- Soothing tea made from chamomile and lavender flowers.

- A candle in a color that is important to your friend.

When you arrive, light the candle and sit down to talk. Make a "feel better" plan that includes a relaxing bath for your friend. Once your friend is in the tub, do some chores for her—wash the dishes, mop the floor, change the bed—something that will make her feel cared-for. Put on water for tea while you're working. When the water boils, make an infusion of chamomile and lavender. When your friend is out of the bath, offer her some soothing tea. Make a wish on the candle so that when she wants to rekindle the warmth of your visit, she can light the candle and feel the love and comfort of a good friend.

Holidays

Yule

Winter Open House Gift

- Yule soap.

- Green votive candles in frosted glass holders.

- Specially decorated holiday hand towel.

Fold the towel so that the decoration shows. Place in the bottom of a decorative cookie tin. Wrap the soaps in something shiny, tie with shiny ribbon. Place the soaps and candles carefully, so they won't bump around too much. Cushion with tissue paper, if desired.

Imbolg

Brigid's Basket

- Imbolg soaps with the two halves unconnected.

- Enough natural twine to string the halves together to create "soap on a rope."

- Fresh rosemary bundles, strung on twine, to perfume the shower.

Tie fresh rosemary branches into small "brooms." To these, attach a loop of natural twine that is long enough to go over a shower head and hang down about two feet.

Include directions on use—thread the soaps onto the string to symbolically "*re*member" them. Loop one rosemary bundle over the showerhead and leave it there. The steam from the shower will release the fresh perfume of rosemary.

Ostara

Brought by a Bunny

- A dozen guest-sized Ostara Soaps.

Form the soaps small, about two ounces each, and make sure they are well-cured. Prepare them about five weeks ahead. Cut spring-themed fabric in 4-inch circles. Wrap the individual soaps, securing the fabric with green raffia, winding it around a few times and tying in a square knot and a bow.

Place the bundles in a basket with a handle. Decorate it by tying a bunch of raffia around the top of the handle. Fluff the raffia to make the bow look full.

On the tag, along with ingredients, magick, and directions for use, write something like: "Tiny bundles of spring energy for you to hide and keep all year long."

Beltane

Rites of Spring

- Beltane soaps.

- Pink and green wash cloths.

- Spring herbs tied in little bouquets to perfume bathwater.

These suggestions make an excellent hostess gift for a May Day party! Roll the soaps lengthwise in the washcloths. Wind ribbons around just as you would wind them around a May Pole. Tie the herbs together in the same way.

On the card, along with the ingredients, intention, and use directions, tell the recipients to put the herb bundles in the tub, to perfume the water, while they enjoy giving each other a bath!

Midsummer

Summer Gathering

- Midsummer soap.

- Sun hat.

- Washcloths, big bath or beach towels, natural sponges.

- Clean, empty 16-ounce yogurt containers.
- Galvanized bucket.

Whether for a weekend or a week, cleaning up will be easier at a Witch camp with this bathing kit. You can put the galvanized bucket right next to the fire to warm the water. Handmade soap is biodegradable, so it's appropriate for fireside wash-ups. Use the old yogurt containers for dipping up rinse water.

Lammas

Harvest Present

- Lammas soap.
- Sisal washcloth.
- Red, yellow, and orange candles.

Wrap the cloths around the soaps, tie with natural twine. Place them with the candles in a pretty, natural-colored basket. Add a loaf of multi-grain bread to complete a thoughtful harvest bounty gift.

Mabon

Pagan Thanksgiving

- Mabon soaps.
- Bundles of fresh sage, rosemary, and parsley.
- Decorative washcloths, with a harvest theme.

Fold the cloths so that the decorations show. Place the soaps on top and tie them together with green ribbon. Tuck the sprigs of fresh herbs into the folds of the cloths. Put everything in a basket of a medium brown color.

On the card, explain that the herbs can be used to perfume the bath or shower. Another use for them is to let them dry, then crumble them into a coarse powder. Add a pinch of crumbled herb to lather from the soap to make a gentle, exfoliating facial scrub!

Samhain

Happy Old and New Year!

- Samhain and Beltane soaps, to demonstrate the balance of opposites.

- One dark- and one light-colored washcloth.

- One dark- and one light-colored candle.

Wrap the Samhain soap in the light washcloth and the Beltane soap in the dark. Tie each with contrasting ribbon and raffia, twisted together to make a multicolored tie. Place everything in a plastic jack-o'-lantern, like those used by kids for trick-or-treating.

On the gift card, along with the ingredients, magickal intentions, and directions for use, include something like, "A New Year's treat for you! Remember the turn of the Wheel all year long."

Epilogue

Some Words From Fellow Magickal Soapmakers

Demetria Clark of Goddess Garden— www.Demetria.com

I do most of my magickal blends in the fall. The fall fills my spirit: being outside, the crisp smells of the earthy air, the warm moist soil moving into place for winter. That smell, I need that smell. I love making magickal blends for friends. They always feel so loved, and they say so when I whip up something special for them, it usually has to do with phone calls and my feelings for them.

I guess for me it is the exchange—the exchange of energy, passion, prayer for the person—keeping the person in my thoughts. Soaps are essential for washing away the world. I started making soap in 1996. I wanted a release. Little did I know that it should have come with a warning sign, "Making soaps leads to an irrational addiction, alights passion, and leads to many other practices." From selling soap, I financed my skin care company that financed my herbal school. We were able to feed our children in lean times and fix our cars when the cost fell outside of the budget. This is a passion of the heart and it becomes a way of life. This passion is empowering. It will not harm me like drugs or alcohol, it teaches me about so much on a daily basis—patience, conservation, self-acceptance, and being okay with the process when something isn't "perfect." That was a big lesson for me, and this "passion" fueled it for me.

Sandra Nash of Fire & Ice SoapWorks—

For me, the craft of cold process soapmaking has been a magickal journey. Long before I began making soap, I felt drawn to do so, although I knew nothing about the process. I had never seen soap made, and I did not know anyone who made soap. It was completely different from anything else I had done in my life. An avid reader, I studied several books, bought equipment and supplies, and took the plunge into soapmaking. I was hooked after turning out my first batch of soap. This is a life's work for me. It is my art, my magick, and my way of connecting with others.

Time slows down when I am making soap. I am an alchemist from long ago, standing over my soap pot, mixing the lye and water with fats and oils. I am always amazed by the transformation as this thin, oily mixture, which at this point is toxic, turns into a rich, creamy swirl to which I add heady essential oils and herbs. When it is ready, I pour it into various molds that are pieces of art on their own. Days later, I cut and trim the hardened mixtures and lay them on specially lined shelves to cure. The scents are intoxicating and permeate my entire house. My patience is rewarded when, after 3 or 4 weeks, I hold finished bars of soap that are gentle on the skin and truly wonderful to look at, smell, and finally, to use.

The old saying, "still waters run deep" applies to me. I appear to be a quiet woman, but soapmaking has made these still waters come to the surface. For it is through the process of concocting my soaps, that I expose my passions and creativity. I want the best ingredients for the soaps that I create. This isn't just about washing hands or getting grime off of your skin. Creating soap that is beautiful to look at, feels good in your hands and on your skin, and smells so good that it makes you breathe more deeply is the goal. Soap such as this shifts your perceptions, even during simple tasks like washing up after gardening.

I think about the people—friends as well as strangers— that will use my soap, and how the energy I've put into the making of the soap connects me to those people. I think of how using that little bar of soap can transform the mundane act of bathing into something special, something magickal. For those few minutes or so that we are in the shower or bath, we can be transported to a Norwegian forest or a field of french lavender or imagine ourselves stepping off a train in some exotic land, with the scents of cinnamon and spices. It can make a bad day better. It can jazz you up or calm you down, depending on what and how you use it. All of this from a little bar of soap—simply magickal.

Cindy Whitaker of Windmill Soaps— *www.WindmillSoaps.com*

Gingerly touching the sides of the kettle, I feel the gentle warmth penetrate my palms. The perfect temperature I have been waiting for has arrived. The other container is in the same comforting zone. Finally, the time for magic has arrived. Slowly I combine the ingredients and stir, as a wonderful batch of handcrafted soap is creating itself right before my eyes. The fragrance of pure soap penetrates my nose, and I know that what is happening for me has been part of history since days long past.

Okay, it isn't magick—it is science—but every time I make soap, it has that thrill of magick. My name is Cindy Whitaker and I have been making handcrafted soap since 1996. "Why would anyone make soap?" you ask. Many reasons come to mind. For me, the pure enjoyment; the knowledge of exactly what is in a product that I am going to apply to my body; the pleasure from handling essential oils; and most definitely, to let my creative self play are some of the reasons.

Handcrafted soap can be made by anyone in his or her kitchen. Only a few special items are needed. Soap is really just a combination of oils (fats), lye, and water. From these basics, you can make soap that is gentle, fragrant, and beautiful. Handcrafted soap bears almost no resemblance to the detergent bars that are commercially produced and sold as "soap" in the market.

The ingredients used in soapmaking are wonderful oils to enhance the gentleness, hardness, texture, cleansing, and lathering ability. Everything you will need to make your own batch of soap can be found in grocery stores, health food stores, and from online suppliers for soap and toiletry makers. Goat milk, honey, oatmeal, aloe vera juice, rosemary, lavender, calendula petals, mints, clays, and pigments are wonderful additions to soap. Essential oils make handcrafted soap all the more interesting in texture and fragrance. Many of these items are also beneficial to your skin. The possibilities are just endless.

Soapmaking has it's own romance and will capture your heart. A good bar of soap will keep you wanting to make more, so do be prepared! And enjoy.

Pamela Baisley of BaisleyHerbals— *www.baisleyherbals.com*

Perhaps because it is such a sensational experience or because the creative process itself is such a mystical one that it is difficult to express to others what happens when you make soap. Making soap...it sounds so simple and straight-forward. But every soapmaker has an incredible passion to perfect his or her own creation, and every cake of soap I make contains that passion and perfection. I describe my hand as a discerning hand that makes, cuts, and wraps every cake of soap. However you describe it, blending oils and ingredients from the Earth—such as garden-grown lemon verbena, lemon balm, and hand-picked leaves from a ginkgo tree—is an individual spiritual experience. That spiritual experience results in beautifully rich, lathering soaps that you offer as gifts for the body and gifts for others to purchase for family and friends. When the process gets to the tracing point and it's almost time to pour the saponifying mixture into its bed, something is completed in me. It isn't just the effect of the fragrant essential oils. Something inside me becomes quite satisfied, as if those who have lived before me have touched me, in gratitude for my dedication to the process of making soap by hand. And on occasion, when my spirit doesn't connect to someone interested in my soaps, I am somewhat reluctant to place the soap into those hands. But when my hand gives a cake to a kindred spirit, well, frankly that's when I tuck an extra bar of soap into the BaisleyHerbals bag. I am truly grateful for that wonderful connection—all due to a cake of soap—and that is my practical way to say "thank you" to whatever forces bring about that moment of understanding and belonging.

Scott Blackson of The Soap Fairy— *www.SoapFairy.com*

Because making soap is my business—and in many ways, my life—my religion absolutely comes through in my work. I am a vegetarian, and have been for 30 years now. I don't eat any animals, as I don't believe I need to kill an animal to be alive, healthy, and well-fed. I don't use tallow or lard in my soaps, as I don't believe I need to kill a cow or pig to make wonderful soap. That is the basis of my business and the reason I started making soap in the first place.

Ironically, when I outgrew my kitchen and went searching for a place to relocate my business, I ended up in a huge warehouse, built as a slaughterhouse in the 1930s. I almost didn't take the space, even though it seemed so perfect (brick floors, with many drains on the floor, high ceilings, huge space, and cheap rent). I did not know how I'd come to work everyday, look up at the tracking running above (where they used to hang the hogs after slaughter), and be able to go about my work. All my vegetarian friends encouraged me to take it. They insisted it was karma balancing, and I should definitely use the space now for something vegetarian and Earth-friendly. They came over and we smudged the plant, stem to stern; did a little ritual apologizing to the many pigs killed there; and promised to use this space for life, not death. The tracking, which once held dead pigs, now sports hanging plants.

Other rituals have become a part of our soapmaking process. I'm a firm believer that you can't make soap in a bad mood. Music is important to me, and I never make a batch of soap without Joni Mitchell singing. (Okay, I'll stretch to Carol King or even James Taylor.) We incubate the soap with an afghan hand-crocheted by my grandmother. I believe everything counts. Many think a blanket is a blanket, but I believe the energy and love that went into making that afghan for me, by a loving grandmother, now goes into that soap when the afghan is placed on top, to keep it warm while it goes through the process of becoming soap.

Anne Harmon of Celestial Body— *www.CelestialBody.com*

All is created in rhythm, with the Earth's beat. As we gather herbs, oils, and hydrosols for our soap making, a candle is lit and this offering is made...

> *To all living things,*
> *to the Earth, our Mother*
> *and to all her children,*
> *we offer stillness and peace, we offer joy and light,*
> *gentleness and love...*
> *with thankfulness...*
> *for to give and receive are one.*
> *As the wonders of Nature swirl and saponify, we infuse*
> *with intent—healing, love, and peace.*

Jo Valerie of Autumn Wind Botanicals— *www.autumnwindbotanicals.com*

I created my first blend of magickal soap when a friend opened a New Age store a little over a year ago. Although talented in many areas, soapmaking had never been her forte (and her schedule didn't allow her to work with it until she got it right). So she asked me if I could "whip up" some soaps of a magickal nature that might be right for her shop and enticing for the clientele.

I truly view my magickal soapmaking as an extension of my spirituality. There is something so deeply satisfying about working with herbs and creating blends that *must* mimic those of our ancestors. The knowledge that I am essentially doing the same work as wise women of old lends an antiquity to the craft. I often visualize those wise women who were respected in their villages and communities, and to whom people came for insight or for that special pouch, herbal blend, or gemstone. Today, people still come for all of those things, but they also come for soap.

Appendix A

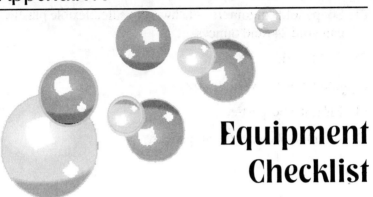

Equipment Checklist

Before you start making magickal soap, check the items on this list to ensure that you have all of the necessary equipment. The last thing you want is to start a batch and realize you've forgotten something!

- ❐ Scale—.25-ounce increments, can reset to zero, able to weigh up to 10 pounds.

- ❐ Two measuring cups—heat-proof glass, 4-cup capacity.

- ❐ Two "easy-read" thermometers

- ❐ Two spoons or spatulas—wooden spoons or one-piece silicone spatulas.

- ❐ Stainless steel measuring cups and spoons.

- ❐ Disposable plastic cup.

- ❐ Rubber gloves.

- ❐ Plastic goggles.
- ❐ White vinegar—put in a spray bottle.
- ❐ Soap mold containers—dishwasher safe, flexible plastic, can hold 24 fluid ounces.
- ❐ Old towel.
- ❐ Glass bowls—various sizes.
- ❐ Mortar and pestle.
- ❐ Bamboo skewers or chopsticks.

Appendix B

Ingredient Shopping List

Use the spaces provided below to keep a "shopping list" of essential oils, herbs, dried flowers, and any other ingredients that you need or would like to try in future magickal soaps. Plan ahead so you will have all of the additives on hand that will be needed in your next batch.

Ingredients to buy:

_____

_____

_____

_____

_____

Ingredients to buy:

_____

_____

_____

_____

_____

_____

_____

_____

_____

_____

_____

_____

_____

_____

Appendix C

Table of Correspondences

This table lists all the ingredients used in this book, as well as properties for some ingredients that are not used in the book. In your own magickal soap, choose additives that impart the properties and magickal qualities you desire.

Property	Essential Oils	Herbs and Flowers	Other Additives
Affection	Rose Ylang Ylang		Orange Flower Water Rosewater
Awakening	Peppermint	Peppermint	
Blessings	Sage	Cedar	
Calming	Chamomile Lavender Geranium		

Property	Essential Oils	Herbs and Flowers	Other Additives
Centering			Benzoin Resin Frankincense Resin
Clarity of Thought	Clary Sage		
Connection to Spirit	Clary Sage		
Courage		Black Pepper	
Deodorizing	Tea Tree		
Earth Energy	Patchouli Vetiver		
Endurance		Black Pepper	
Energy	Orange Peppermint	Peppermint	
Focus	Clary Sage Orange Peppermint		
Feminine Balance	Clary Sage		
Gentleness	Chamomile Lavender		
Happiness	Orange		
Harmony			
Healing		Borage Comfrey Yarrow	Oatmeal

Property	Essential Oils	Herbs and Flowers	Other Additives
Home		Cinnamon	Oatmeal
Love	Rose Jasmine YlangYlang	Rose Ylang Ylang	Orange Flower Water Rosewater
Masculine Energy	Peppermint	Peppermint	
Meditation			
Menstruation	Clary Sage Lavender		
Mental Attunement			
Moon Energy	Lemon	Mugwort	
Partnership	Rose		
Protection	Black Pepper Sage		
Relaxation	Chamomile Lavender		
Release of Sorrow		Dandelion Mint	
Rest	Lavender Chamomile	Lavender Chamomile	
Sleep-inducing	Lavender Chamomile	Lavender Chamomile	

Property	Essential Oils	Herbs and Flowers	Other Additives
Soothing	Chamomile Lavender Geranium	Borage Lavender Chamomile	
Strength	Cedar Pine		
Sun energy	Orange	Annatto Seed Cinnamon	
Wellness	Lavender	Black Pepper	
Wishes		Elder Flowers	

Appendix D

Pure Olive Oil Soap

You can make an excellent soap using just olive oil. The soap will have a low lather and feel slippery. It is quite gentle, and the bars get very hard. It will take considerably longer to trace than the Basic Recipe used throughout the book.

2 oz.   lye
6 oz.   water
16 oz. olive oil

Prepare the lye solution, and heat the oil. Stir together as usual. Pour at medium to full trace. Insulate as usual. Wearing gloves and eye protection, check the soap in a few hours. If some oil has separated, give it a good stir with the spatula. Cover it and wait another eight hours. If there is more oil, which is not likely, stir again. The soap will initially be very sticky, so wait an extra day before removing it from the mold.

Put it in the freezer overnight if it looks like it won't pop out of the mold on its own. Cut and shape and cure the bars as normal. The soap will become very hard in about three weeks. Soap made with only olive oil is very prone to dissolving, so be absolutely certain to keep it out of water between uses.

Appendix E

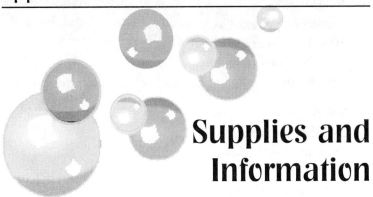

Supplies and Information

Camden-Grey Essential Oils

3591 NW 82 Ave.
Miami, FL 33122
877-232-7662 or 305-500-9630
www.camdengrey.com

Glad Rags/Keepers!Inc.

PO Box 12648
Portland, OR 97212
800-799-4523 or 503-282-0436
www.gladrags.com
Cotton menstrual pads, menstrual sea sponges, etc.

Herb Products Company

11012 Magnolia Blvd.
PO Box 898
North Hollywood, CA 91603-0898
800-877-3104 or 818-761-0351
www.herbproducts.com
Enormous selection of herbs at reasonable prices.

Jardin du Soliel

3932 Sequim Dungeness Way
Sequim, WA 98382
877-527-3461
www.JardinduSoliel.com
Small Lavender farm in Sequim, Washington. Essential oil, dried lavender, and lavender gifts.

Majestic Mountain Sage

918 West 700 North, Ste. 104
Logan, UT 84321
435-755-0863
Fax: 435-755-2108
www.The-sage.com
Comprehensive soapmaking supplies.

Mint Meadow Country Oils

Deb Shuman
112 Schreier Dr.
Camp Douglas, WI 54618
608-427-3561
http://members.tripod.com/~mintmeadow
dshuman@mwt.net
Organic mint and mint-blend essential oils.

Natural Oils International

9243 Cranford Ave.
Arleta, CA 91331-4309
www.naturaloils.com
Supplier of high-quality base oils.

Oberon Design

1813 Empire Industrial Ct.
Santa Rosa, CA 95403
www.oberondesign.com
Sales@oberondesign.com
Beautiful leather-bound journals.

Rainbow Meadow Inc.

310 Cooper St.
Jackson MI 49201
517-817-0021 or 800-207-4047
Fax: 517-817-0026
www.rainbowmeadow.com
Essential oils and other supplies for soapmaking.

Sweetcakes Soapmaking Supplies

www.Sweetcakes.com
info@sweetcakes.com
952-945-9900
Fax: 952-945-9905
Tested, soap-safe fragrance oils. Source for the rose fragrance used in this book. (Sweetcakes sells both natural and synthetic fragrances. Be sure to note that unless "Natural Fragrance Oil" or "Pure Essential Oil," is stated, fragrance contains synthetic substances.)

Tenzing Momo

93 Pike Street
Seattle, WA 98101
206-623-9837
www.tenzingmomo.com
Magickal herbs, essential oils, and other additives.

Appendix F

Selected Titles From My Library

Budapest, Zsuzsanna E. *The Grandmother of Time: A Woman's Book of Celebrations, Spells, and Sacred Objects for Every Month of the Year*. New York, NY: Harper San Francisco, 1989.

Campanelli, Pauline. Dan Campanelli, Illustrator. *Wheel of the Year: Living the Magical Life*. St. Paul, MN: Llewellyn Publications 1989.

Coney, Norma. *The Complete Soapmaker: Tips, Techniques & Recipes for Luxurious Handmade Soaps*. Asheville, NC: Lark Books, 1997.

Coss, Melinda. Emma Peios, Photographer. *The Handmade Soap Book*. Pownal, VT: Storey Books, 1998.

Cunningham, Scott. *Cunningham's Encyclopedia of Magical Herbs*. St. Paul, MN: Llewellyn Publications, 1985.

——. *Wicca: A Guide for the Solitary Practitioner*. St. Paul, MN: Llewellyn Publications, 1990.

Dunwich, Gerina. *The Wicca Garden: A Modern Witch's Book of Magickal and Enchanted Herbs and Plants*. New York, NY: Citadel Library of the Mystic Arts, 1996.

Evert-Hopman, Ellen. *A Druid's Herbal for the Sacred Earth Year*. Rochester, VT: Destiny Books, 1995.

Maine, Sandy. *The Soap Book : Simple Herbal Recipes*. Loveland, CO: Interweave Press, 1995.

Miller-Cavitch, Susan. *The Natural Soap Book: Making Herbal and Vegetable-Based Soaps*. Pownal, VT: Storey Books, 1995.

——. *The Soapmaker's Companion: A Comprehensive Guide With Recipes, Techniques & Know-How*. Pownal, VT: Storey Books, 1997.

Moura, Ann (Aoumiel). *Green Witchcraft: Folk Magic, Fairy Lore & Herb Craft*. St. Paul, MN: Llewellyn Publications, 1996.

Starhawk. *The Spiral Dance: A Rebirth of the Ancient Religion of the Great Goddess*. San Francisco, CA: Harper San Francisco, 1999.

Watson, Nancy B. *Practical Solitary Magic*. York Beach, ME: Samuel Weiser, 1996.

Appendix G

Sources Found or to Investigate

In this book, I have provided a number of online supply sources, as well as recommended books. Use the following spaces to keep a list of Websites, books, the contact information of people you meet, and other sources you have found useful in your Magickal Soapmaking quest or that you would like to investigate further.

_____

_____

_____

_____

_____

_____

Appendix H

Special Occasion List

Use this list to fill in the names of important people and events that you definitely don't want to forget! Keep track of all the occasions you will be attending, and plan ahead to give special gifts of magickal soap appropriate to the occasion.

Person/Event	Date	Location	Notes

Person/Event	Date	Location	Notes

Appendix I

Soap Grimoire Worksheet

Use the chart below as a template for entries in your Soap Grimoire. This will enable you to record all of the important details and information about each batch of magickal soap, for future reference.

Recipe: _____

Date: _____

Estimated cured date: _____

Specifics of the purpose of the batch:

_____

_____

_____

Approximate temperature of the work area: _____
     Was is raining? Dry? Humid?

_____

What was the Moon phase? _____
     In what sign? _____

What was the Sun Sign? _____

What time of day did you work? _____

How did you stir? _____

How long did it take to trace? _____

What happened as you added each ingredient?

_____

_____

_____

_____

_____

Cure notes:

_____

_____

_____

_____

_____

Use notes:

_____

_____

_____

_____

_____

Packaging notes:

_____

_____

_____

_____

_____

Gift notes:

_____

_____

_____

_____

_____

Additional:

_____

_____

Appendix J

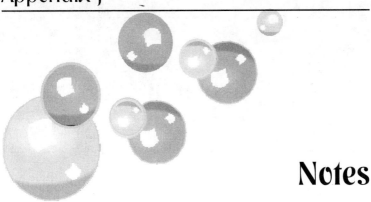

Notes

If you have not yet started your own personal Soap Grimoire, or if there are just some particular notes you would like to keep handy for yourself right within the covers of this book, use these pages.

_____

_____

_____

_____

_____

_____

_____

Notes:

Talisman → object considered 2 possess
Amulet → Supernatural or magical powers
Could Be a sentimenal object
use
these
2 put on the front of your GRIMOIRE

Notes:

Notes:

Index

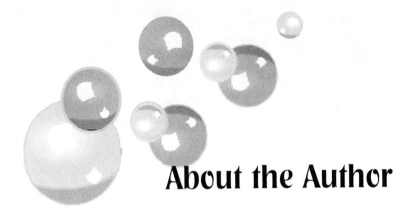

About the Author

Alicia Grosso is a soapmaker, teacher, and Witch. She has a lifelong interest in magick, herbs, and handcrafts. She has studied and practiced Earth Mysteries for more than 20 years. She's been creating handmade soap and toiletries for seven years.

Alicia is the owner and Creative Director of the Annabella and Company Creativity Collective. She lives in Los Angeles with her very clean husband and their companion animals.

Alicia teaches classes and workshops in soapmaking. For more information, please go to *www.MagicalSoap.com*.